Partners
in Spirit

Bahá'í Publishing
415 Linden Avenue, Wilmette, Illinois 60091-2844

Printed in the United States of America on acid-free paper ∞

09   08   07   06   4   3   2   1

Cardin, Heather.
    Partners in spirit : what couples say about marriages that work /
by Heather Cardin.
        p. cm.
    Includes bibliographical references and index.
    ISBN-13: 978-1-931847-31-5 (alk. paper)
    ISBN-10: 1-931847-31-2 (alk. paper)
        1. Marriage—Religious aspects—Bahai Faith. 2. Family—
Religious aspects—Bahai
    Faith. 3. Married people—Interviews. I. Title.

    BP388.M37C37 2006
    297.9'3441—dc22

                                                    2006049857

Cover design by Tracy Heckel of Guten Tag! www.gutentag.us
Book design by Suni D. Hannan

Partners
in Spirit

What Couples Say About
Marriages That Work

By
Heather Cardin

Bahá'í
PUBLISHING
Wilmette, IL

Contents

Chapter 1
Spiritual Foundations
and Emotional Development

Chapter 2
Love

Chapter 3
Family and Consent

Chapter 4
Expressing Sexuality

Chapter 5
Children

For my parents,
Ron & Edna Nablo,
&
for my husband, Bernie

Acknowledgments

This book could not have been written without the extraordinary candor, perseverance, courage, patience, intelligence and humor of some remarkable people. I would like to express my gratitude to the many couples and individuals who shared their stories with me. In particular, I would like to remember June Barrow, who wrote to me shortly before her untimely death from cancer. My deep appreciation goes to each of those listed below.

I also offer sincere gratitude to Terry Cassiday at *Bahá'í Publishing* for inviting me to submit the early drafts of the book, and for her encouragement. It has been a joy to work with her. Christopher Martin has been an invaluable editor, whose patience, kindness, and meticulous attention to detail were superb. I thank him from my heart. I also thank Bahhaj Taherzadeh, who has cast his careful eye over the manuscript. In its initial stages, my niece, Audrey Batterham, went over each page with comments and a thorough first-draft edit. Thanks, Audrey.

This book has been several years in the preparation. My children were in their early teens when I began. They are now young adults. They went through their adolescence with their mother's divided attention. Any words of thanks to them would be inadequate to express how grateful I am that they learned to be patient with me saying, "Wait, I'm writing!" To Melodie, Maya, and Jesse: I love you.

Thank You:

June and Reginald Barrow
Jameson (Jamie) Bond
Carol and David Bowie
Muguette and Peter Brady
David and Haodan (Mary) Brown
Margaret Bremner and Bruce Filson
Diana and Don Dainty
Andrea and Stephen Doran
Cheryl and Gordon Epp
Edward Epp
David Erickson and Belinda Forsee
Karin Ferguson
Robin Goertz
Coral and Ovidio Gomez
Nahid and Rick Gordon
Ann and David Hall
Baxter Huston
Wendy James
Ali and Tracy Khajavi
Ahkivgak Kiana

Ginny and Greg Kintz
Bob LeBlanc and Louise Profeit-LeBlanc
Phoebe Anne and William Lemmon
Ho-San and Mariette Leong
Bea and Clyde MacTavish
Manuel Marcial
Pierre Martel
Helen de Marsh and Maury Miloff
Susan Eghrari Moraes
Gillian and Parviz Mottahed
Edna and Ron Nablo
Stuart North
Hélène and Dr. Thavil (Tony) Panalaks
Arnold and Junia Perreault
Bibiane and Emile Perreault
David and Marilee Rhody
Elizabeth Rochester
Suzanne Schuurman
Pat and Sandy Slobodian
Barry and Marilyn Smith
Jeff and Pam Stellick
Margaret Varner
Sylvia and Yovanny Vasquez
Janis Zrudlo

*And when He desired to manifest grace **and** beneficence to men, and to set the world in order, He revealed observances and created laws; among them He established the law of marriage, made it as a fortress for well-being and salvation, and enjoined it upon us in that which was sent down out of the heaven of sanctity in His Most Holy Book. He saith, great is His glory: "Enter into wedlock, O people, that ye may bring forth one who will make mention of Me amid My servants; this is my bidding unto you; hold fast to it as an assistance to yourselves."*

Bahá'u'lláh

PUBLISHER'S PREFACE

The institution of marriage holds an exalted position in the Bahá'í Faith. The Bahá'í Faith teaches that marriage is a spiritual partnership between a husband and wife and that it is designed to help both of them grow spiritually. Hence, it is a sacred bond that continues not only in this world but also in the world after death.

The Bahá'í Faith is the youngest of the world's independent religions. Born in Persia in the mid-nineteenth century, it has since spread to virtually every corner of the earth. Today, its membership represents what may well be the most ethnically and culturally diverse organized association of people. The growth of the Faith has been fueled by a body of teachings that its followers regard as the Revelation of God's guidance for the collective coming of age of humankind: the oneness of the human race, the oneness of the world's religions as the principal civilizing force in history, and the imperative challenge facing the earth's inhabitants to construct a global society based on principles of unity and justice.

The Founder of the Faith, Bahá'u'lláh, received His revelation from God after being imprisoned by the Persian authorities for affirming the exalted position of a merchant called the Báb ("Gate"). The Báb claimed to be a Messenger of God—such as Moses, Jesus, and Muḥammad—who had come to prepare the way for another Messenger of God who would unite the peoples of the world. Shortly after the Báb was martyred by the Persian authorities, Bahá'u'lláh and His family were forced to endure a series of banishments—first to Baghdád, then to Constantinople (present-day Istanbul), then to Adrianople, and finally to the prison-city of 'Akká, located in what is now Israel.

It was in Baghdád that Bahá'u'lláh declared that He was the Messenger of God foretold by the Báb. Like the Messengers of God before Him, He had come to renew the teachings of God on earth. His mission was to guide humanity into a new era of world peace.

After Bahá'u'lláh passed away, He appointed His son, 'Abdu'l-Bahá, to succeed Him as the head of the new faith. 'Abdu'l-Bahá guided the Bahá'í Faith for thirty years, and upon his passing he designated his grandson, Shoghi Effendi, to lead the faith. Shoghi Effendi then led the new religion for thirty-six years, and several years after his passing, the Universal House of Justice—the present head of the Bahá'í Faith—was elected.

The present book is yet another attempt to bring the teachings of the Bahá'í Faith to the general public. It is hoped that, after reading the Bahá'í teachings on marriage, the reader will be inspired to dig deeper into the writings of the Bahá'í Faith.

INTRODUCTION

Marriage, among the mass of the people, is a physical bond,
and this union can only be temporary, since it is foredoomed to
a physical separation at the close.

'Abdu'l-Bahá

This is a book about what makes marriages work. It is written
from a perspective that includes spiritual life because the majority of the people who agreed to be interviewed believe that
spirituality is an important component of marital success.
Many of those interviewed are members of the Bahá'í Faith.
Some originally came from a variety of religious backgrounds—such as Christian, Jewish, Muslim, and Buddhist—
while others were born into Bahá'í families. Many elements of
their stories are useful for anyone interested in how happily
married couples approach their marriages on a daily basis.

The Bahá'í Faith teaches this construct: peace is inevitable.
Such a belief may appear utopian, but Bahá'ís are convinced
that with work, love, and time, this world will become a better place, and they dedicate their lives to this goal. Their
hope is founded, in part, on a statement of 'Abdu'l-Bahá—
the son and appointed successor of the faith's Prophet and
founder, Bahá'u'lláh—as he laid the first stone of the Bahá'í
Temple in Wilmette, Illinois, in 1912. He said, placing the
stone, "The Temple is already built." The physical temple,
of course, took many years to build, and the story of its con-
struction is replete with the victories that come with vision
and hard work. He was, as he deposited the stone in the
place where it still rests, seeing the future, and he was seeing
it with confidence. He taught, in that moment, a spiritual

principle in practical action—the ideal, as stated by his father, Bahá'u'lláh, to "see the end in the beginning."[1]

Marriage is such a vision. When two people marry, they undertake to see the end as it begins: to see their lives unfold together, regardless of what happens. The temple of their marriage is built, piece by piece, stage by stage. Several years ago, as I thought of marriage in this fashion, I wondered about the building blocks of marriages. So I asked forty-three couples about their apparent success in their marriages. Their responses were articulate, thoughtful, and insightful. Some people were working in a second or third language and still managed to share their perspectives with clarity and fluency. I collected the couples' stories through "snail-mail," email, telephone interviews, and face-to-face interviews.

The stories came from all over the world. For all who wanted them, I offered a list of nineteen "guiding questions" that I had developed for the respondents to use. The questions were:

1. Why do you think your marriage is successful?
2. Are there spiritual principles or values that you feel have been particularly useful or of assistance to your success in marriage?
3. How important was / is consultation?
4. How do you deal with anger with each other or with others? Please share other emotions and their effects.
5. How have children affected your relationship, if applicable?
6. Is money a pressure?

8. How important is sexual attraction?

9. How many years have you been married to this person? How did you "know?"

10. How have you changed, independently or with each other?

11. How much, if at all, do you "rely" on each other?

12. Do you consider your marriage an "easy" one or is it successful because of a lot of "work?"

13. How did your own childhood affect your expectations and perceptions of marriage? For example, do you think your view on this subject is different according to when, or where, you were born and raised, such as the 1950s in Canada compared with the 1980s in Africa?

14. Has your relationship been affected by the media?

15. What habits or practices have contributed to the success of your marriage?

16. How do you deal with household tasks?

17. Are there changes or evolutions which have been critical to your marriage?

18. Have you ever considered separation and divorce, and if so, how did you manage to "stick it out?"

My last question asked couples to comment spontaneously on any areas that they felt I might have omitted. In retrospect, I would eliminate question 14, the media question, since everyone who replied to it indicated that it was not an issue, and replace it with a question about culture. Some couples shared very similar cultural backgrounds, while others commented on how adapting to different heritages could be both an enriching and a challenging experience. Almost all the couples described marriage as a process, something built from the ground up.

As Karin Ferguson, a Canadian recently returned from Belize, put it, "My husband Ian and I have been married fifty years. This is an amazing feat no matter which way one looks at it—as most people today just don't think of doing anything for fifty years. . . ."

We are all too aware of the many things that can derail the hopefulness of a wedding ceremony. Divorce statistics speak eloquently to loss of vision. What the hopeful couple believes, aspires for, and promises, does not happen. This tends to make people believe that it is not possible, really, to be happily married, and they lose confidence in the concept of marriage. Many, of course, decide not to marry and simply move in with one another. For Bahá'ís—as well as others who believe in chastity before marriage—this is not an option. The central metaphor for marriage in the Bahá'í teachings is that marriage should be "a fortress for well-being" for the married couple.[2] Within this fortress, the couple is able to live together in mutual happiness, and they are able to withstand the many hardships that often drive unmarried couples apart.

The couples and individuals who shared their stories with me for this book spoke frankly from the point of view of the most powerful teacher: experience. They have, for the most part, been married to one person for a long time, and after enduring many struggles and challenges, have come to believe that there are some strategies that are useful for married couples and for couples considering marriage. The single most important theme that emerged from the interviews appeared to be the initial commitment to staying married. For most of these couples, their marriage has always been their first priority. They stay married because they want to be married to each other.

Pressures may arise that disturb the equilibrium and joy of a marriage, such as challenges with relatives and children, money problems, sexual dysfunction, attraction to others, or interference from others. There is a litany of documented problems. This is not a book about problems. Nor is it a "how to" book. Simply, it is a book that believes in the power of example. This book builds its stories around success.

We have all been in a group—perhaps a dinner, a party, or other social gathering—where people tell their "story." A couple is asked, "How did you fall in love," or "How did you meet," and a story unfolds. Often, it is told in a different fashion by the wife and by her husband. Sometimes, they speak in tandem. Sometimes, one will interject. There is often a lot of laughter.

The couples who have contributed their stories to this book have done so frankly. There has been laughter and some tears. Some stories came to me poignantly; June Barrow died of cancer shortly after she and Reginald sent their twenty-fourth-anniversary reflections. Tony Panalaks also passed away, in the winter of 2006.

Although these stories come from people who have integrated spiritual life into their daily routine, I believe that there are commonalities that are applicable to people from all walks of life. In some of these marriages, both spouses are members of the Bahá'í faith. Others are "mixed," whether by holding differing religious convictions, coming from different cultures and races, or finding new models of marriage after having experienced a previous alliance that did not work. Many of the couples have chosen to be "pioneers" for the Bahá'í faith, leaving their homes in order to support the work of Bahá'í communities in a variety of locales around the globe. Thus, you find Americans in Honduras, Canadians in Belize, Australians in Papua New Guinea, or Europeans in Labrador.

The spiritual underpinnings of many of these marriages is the topic of the first chapter. However, I was more interested in each aspect of life that the couples felt had contributed to the success of their marriages. This was my primary curiosity: to find out how these various individuals, heralding from different countries, representing different generations, and almost all sharing the common factor of having been married—happily, by their own definition—for a long time, had met with success.

The couples who share their stories here have made a choice, and they have committed to staying with the person they have chosen. They are married and have been married happily for a long time. This is a book about hope. The perspectives here are from marriages where the partners have worked hard at staying married and still care deeply for one another. Some of these marriages continue to "struggle," but the couples are committed to success, and they believe in it. When asked, "Why is your marriage successful?," consistently, their replies were that failure was not an option. Most people believed in the possibility that the marriage with this person could be forever, not just "till death do you part" but "in all the worlds of God."[3]

Their bond, in most cases, was anchored firmly in shared spiritual beliefs, but the practices of those beliefs were widely varied, and the self-expression was diverse. Sometimes the husband thought the marriage worked for one reason, and the wife for another. Some things were hard to put a finger on: what attracted one person to another always contained some element of mystery, although many of the couples spoke about the role of "destiny." The stories are not always the same within the marriage, but sometimes they are exactly the same, and it is the unity of vision itself to which the couple's success is attributed.

What is clear from these personal narratives is that happy marriages can be achieved. There seem to be certain "ingredients" for a successful marriage. These marriages work. They do not simply work at an automatic level—they bring joy to the partners. They are based in spirit and in love.

My questions led to comments on finances, sexuality, family, and the future. Marriages tended to go through cycles; they endured because of hard work and commitment. The marriages you will meet here are meant to inspire, encourage, and assist in your own marriages, hopes, and dreams. There is no magic formula, but these accounts show clearly that marriage can be "a fortress for well-being." Or, as my eldest daughter puts it, laughingly, "Marriage for dummies."

Here are the stories.

1

SPIRITUAL FOUNDATIONS AND EMOTIONAL DEVELOPMENT

*When, therefore, the people of Bahá undertake to marry,
the union must be a true relationship, a spiritual
coming together as well as a physical one, so that
throughout every phase of life, and in all the
worlds of God, their union will endure; for this
real oneness is a gleaming out of the love of God.*

'Abdu'l-Bahá

It is difficult to define spirituality. It is also somewhat challenging to examine our own emotional development. Sometimes the two seem quite interconnected, and at other times, they seem independent of one another. In this chapter, the individuals I interviewed offered various perspectives on how marriage is an aspect of both spiritual growth and emotional change.

Spirituality and Marriage

I was interested in exploring the effect of a "spiritual" perspective on the success of marriages, and what that meant. Ovidio Gomez of Honduras articulated the idea most concisely: "Every time I feel closer to God, or that I am growing spiritually, I feel more love and want to be closer to my wife Coral."

Susan Eghrari Moraes is of Persian origin but has lived in Brazil all her life. She offered an interesting analogy in her exploration of her happy marriage:

When I think of my marriage, a classic example comes to my mind. When I was in the fifth grade, my math teacher introduced a new subject to the class—the intersection points between two circles. He drew two separate circles on the board, each with its own individuality and characteristics. The next stage consisted of drawing the intersection points between the circles. They continued to have their own identity, but after a certain moment the two circles mingled one with the other, and within that shared area, the teacher applied a different texture that was common to both circles. The more the centers of each circle came closer to each other, the wider the area of intersection became.

Susan's analogy makes me think of spirituality as a circular force, the intersection of two individual circles coming together. The idea that marriage has a spiritual component is not unique to the Bahá'í teachings; however, the application of "spirituality" to marriage has many definitions. Another couple, Ginny and Greg Kintz, Americans then living in Africa, also used a geometric analogy to describe the success of their marriage: "Fundamentally, our marriage works because, in spite of the differences in our individual interests, career choices, habits, and so on, we have a common vision of our purpose in life. The 'triangle analogy' has proven to be completely true in our marriage. This is the illustration in which God is the apex of the triangle and the other two points represent the marriage partners. As the partners individually draw closer to God, the result is that they grow closer to each other."

At the time of this writing, Greg and Ginny have been married "twenty-seven wonderful years." They note, "We talked about the future, and it was mutual dreams and goals— when we couldn't imagine the future without being together."

Service and Marriage

Service was another important aspect for several of the married couples I interviewed. The Kintzes emphasized service to their faith as an important component in their marriage:

> Our primary, mutual goal is service to our faith. We go about it differently and serve in different ways, but we both recognize this as the purpose of our being. Everything else is secondary. We include maintaining a strong marriage and happy family life in our definition of service. Faith needs strong families, and thus the time that we take for just being together as a family is, for us, time spent as service. We learned about the importance of family time from a Bahá'í couple that we looked to as role models. This family time has been extremely important, both for our marriage and for building the strong bond that we have with our children.

Helen de Marsh, in telling the story of how she and Maury Miloff decided to marry, offered several insights into the importance of a "spiritual coming together" during courtship. Helen, a Bahá'í who chose her faith in young adulthood, said, "Maury had these round John Lennon glasses, an afro, and piercing eyes. He impressed me with his knowledge and his analytical skills; boy, could he hold forth on just about any topic! We cast about for a way to be of service. We decided then that we would go to St. Pierre and Miquelon together on the French Immersion Program the following summer. As it turned out the program was full, but Maury showed his usual tenacity and kept calling the director in the hope of a cancellation."

The idea of serving their faith together is one that has cemented the connection of many people who pursue their spiritual beliefs as a component of courtship. Helen continued the story:

I found myself in the fog, landing in a tiny plane on this rocky bit of an island which was something out of my wildest dreams. It was France, but it was Newfoundland all at once. Men in berets would go out on bikes to gather the loaves at dawn to start the new day, just as the fishermen were setting out for the catch. Naturally, I was swept overboard by this truly amazing man in that surreal place. The moment of truth came for our relationship and I found myself alone, walking the streets of St. Pierre in the densest fog, repeating the Tablet of Ahmad* and considering our future. I had weighed my requirements with myself, and during the prayer reverie I experienced a sense of confirmation that is indescribable. Let me just say it was as if the gates of heaven opened and we were as good as married in my heart and mind.

I was interested to note that Helen suggested, in this part of her narrative, that she had "requirements" when looking for a marriage partner. Many people have an invisible wish list, and one of the themes that emerged from the stories I was hearing in preparing this book was that often, couples would discover during the course of their marriage that what they had thought were their requirements had undergone

---

* Written work of Bahá'u'lláh that is often used as a comfort during difficult times.

change, or that their spouse was a different person from whom they had thought. Helen added a bit more to this story: "The next day I met the poor bewildered Maury, whom I had been cold-shouldering somewhat, and told him that it was a done deal! We sat and gazed out at the Atlantic Ocean and read The Seven Valleys (a Bahá'í text) through, and more than that, we understood it!"

To some readers, it may be very strange to think of a newly-engaged couple celebrating their engagement by reading scriptures from their religion. To others, it will appear quite normal. Helen's story indicates that couples who value a spiritual component in their married lives will rely on the principles of their faith to help them realize and appreciate the purpose of their marriage. Helen noted that despite the joy she and Maury were experiencing about their decision to marry, there were other issues at stake. She stated, "My parents were not so excited to hear this news, which may have something to do with the fact that I was nineteen, a new convert to a different religion, and not through my first degree—never mind without a career established for myself. Also, this person was of a different background and was newly adhering to this unknown faith that I had chosen as well. It was all a lot to absorb."

Spiritual Courtship

Another couple spoke about the spiritual component of courtship. This couple provides the sole exception to those in this book regarding longevity of marriage. They have not been married very long. However, David Brown's story of his courtship was very interesting to me, in view of the differences between the cultures mentioned in his story. David traveled to China to teach English and to help support Bahá'í communities there. He had no intention of seeking a wife while in China, yet he wrote me a long description of how he came to know Haodan, who is known also as Mary. She had recently become a Bahá'í and had offered to teach language classes to assist the settlement of Bahá'ís who were traveling to China for service. David told the following story of their courtship: "When we started classes, I felt a little bad because she would teach me for two or three hours straight and would never accept any pay for her services. I finally came up with a way to indicate my gratitude while at the same time get to know and spend more time with her. I would take her out for dinner or lunch after our class. Over two months and many McDonalds meals (one of the only Western restaurants in Changchun) I really felt like I had gotten to know her well and was interested in pursuing a relationship that was more than just friends."

The Bahá'í teachings on marriage state that a person should "become thoroughly acquainted with the character" of the person with whom he is considering marriage.[1] David speaks to the process, for him and for Mary, in China:

I had the idea that she also was interested in me, so one evening over pizza I indicated that I liked her a lot, and I asked her if she liked me. To my relief she said yes. I then said I was hoping that we could investigate each other's characters to see if we were compatible with each other for marriage. This confused her a little and she asked me if this meant I wanted to be her boyfriend. I said, "No, not really." I told her that we would investigate to see if we wanted to marry one another but would not really be boyfriend and girlfriend. This confused and upset her because at first I said I liked her, and then said I did not want to be her boyfriend.

The evening wound up badly. I thought it was good the way I had put it, with no expectations or commitment, but because of cultural differences and our different backgrounds, she did not see it in this way.

After a few days of not talking to her, I could not stand it any more so called her up and asked her out for a walk. That evening, I apologized to her about what I had said the previous evening and said that basically, I really did want to be her boyfriend. She did not believe me. We walked all over Changchun that evening and I finally convinced her that I really did like her and I genuinely wanted her to be my girlfriend.

Over the next week, we met for long hours every day and talked about everything. We talked about our future aspirations, how many children we wanted (it had never occurred to her that she could have more than one child) and what we imagined our wedding would be like.

I felt like I had known her so well from before and that over the week we had become so close that I asked her how close she thought she was to deciding that she wanted to marry me. She answered that she was 70% sure that she wanted to marry me. I was elated. If she was 70% sure after one week, it would only be a few more days before she felt fully ready to marry me! I was very excited but managed to wait an entire week and I asked her again. She said 72%. I was surprised to say the least. It took her one week to feel 70% sure and the next week, only 2% more. I took heart that at least there was a little progress and decided to be patient for another week. At the end of the third week she said 71%. I felt deflated and did not know what to do. Things started to get bad.

Many courtships can go awry for one reason or another. Communication can be critical, so the narrative of two people working in two languages and from two different cultural backgrounds was particularly intriguing.

As David narrated, "Things continually deteriorated until one evening, after a big argument on the phone, it ended up that we said maybe we should just forget about thinking about marriage at all. I was devastated."

David went to a friend for advice. He recounted,

I asked her why things did not work out. I had been so devoted to Mary and had loved her unconditionally. Jo tried to console me, but nothing helped me feel better. That cold night I walked home at about 12:30 am. I was alone on the street, and I just wept. I cried out to God and asked why this had happened. As if in answer to my prayer I was hit with a realization. The love I had had for Mary was not really unconditional. If it was unconditional, I would not have gotten upset if she needed more time to make up her mind. I would not have even been upset if she did not want to spend time with me or be my girlfriend anymore. If I loved her unconditionally, her happiness would be what mattered most, and if she was happiest to just remain friends, then I should feel happy for her and not sad for myself.

I found this a surprising amount of detachment in someone so young. David and Mary shared a little more in their own version of "happily ever after." David said, "I immediately went home and wrote her an e-mail, expressing what I had realized. No matter what, I was going to be happy and thankful for the time we did get to spend with one another and just be detached. I was going to enjoy my time with her, and have no expectations."

I'm not sure how David accomplished this, but he said,

As soon as I started to do this, our relationship began improving, and after a few months we decided to marry each other. We have joyfully committed to spending and enjoying the rest of eternity with one another, continually supporting and helping each other grow.

Over the past few years, we have had a lot of tests and challenges, especially over cultural differences, but both of us try to serve and support one another before thinking of ourselves, and by always trying to remain detached and happy, we have grown closer and more devoted to one another. The greatest advice I can give to those who are thinking about getting married to someone is to truly investigate his or her character to see if he or she is compatible with you. Do not go into marriage thinking you can change your spouse or that your spouse will change on his or her own. It is most probable that they will not change very much, so it is very important to truly know your partner before committing to marriage.

The admonition to choose one's partner carefully was echoed in other stories. Many of the people who shared their views spoke about the importance of taking personal responsibility for their own actions. The individuals tried not to have expectations that would cause disappointment if the partner did not fulfill them. This involved being very self-aware even during the process of finding a husband or wife. It was not a question of "falling in love," although some of the couples certainly felt that they had fallen in love with their partner. Many, however, were looking for specific characteristics in a potential spouse. For example, Edna Nablo explained what she had been looking for in a marriage partner:

> I don't think I can answer these questions without some background of what I was looking for in a marriage partner. Perhaps an incident from high school can easily illustrate some of my thinking. There was a girl who sat next to me in class (always dressed to the nines, and always in the latest fashion) who became engaged to one of the football heroes. She talked at length about how they danced so perfectly together, and nothing that she said about him seemed to have more substance than this. Now, I love to dance, and I know the exhilaration that comes when you are dancing in the arms of someone whose dance steps are perfectly synchronized with yours, but I also knew that the probability was that after marriage, the likelihood that you would spend a lot of time dancing was pretty small, so you had better look for something more telling than this when making a choice.

Consultation in Marriage

The theme of consultation also emerged from the interviews I had with married couples.

Peter and Muguette Brady, whose marriage united an American with a French Canadian, noted the importance of consultation as a component of marital success. Peter said, "Our marriage works because we work at it. We have common or similar goals and interests. Before we married, we practiced consultation and set a pattern that continues. We do not let things simmer, and we limit recriminations. Our arguments do not include attacks on the other person or dredge up events or words said years ago as part of our present argument. Usually we consult and try to work out any challenges this way. I know that I want this marriage to work and to be a happy marriage and will do what is necessary to keep it going."

The need to be able to consult successfully with one's partner was confirmed by Stephen and Andrea Doran. Andrea had been very young when the Dorans were married, just before her eighteenth birthday. Steve is almost a decade older. They spent many of the earlier years of their marriage, while raising their five children, in isolated communities, where Steve was a nurse. Their ability to communicate became critical, with family support quite distant. They were a couple who felt that to "take counsel together in secret" was very important to the consultative process and that the commitment to work out different views would be an important theme for success in marriage.[2]

This sense of privacy in consultation was an important note for many couples, which seemed an important reinforcement in the commitment to their marriage. They learned to resolve small differences together without making large issues out of small ones. Carol and David Bowie noted,

A few years later we began to realize that we certainly perceived the world from different perspectives! I squeezed the toothpaste tube and he rolled it. I put toilet tissue and paper towels so the paper came over the top—and, you guessed it, he mounted them to come from under the back! I put my clothes in the laundry or on a chair at night, while his were dropped where he stood. Instructions for the assembly of toys, furniture, and so on didn't mean the same thing to both of us either. How we dealt with these now insignificant differences became the model for our ability to solve problems and face life's serious challenges such as illness and death.

Our biggest challenges, which we steadfastly faced together, were the deaths of our one-day-old son in 1963 and then our thirty-five-year-old daughter in 1995. A very big lesson we learned through the gradual awareness of our opposite qualities or views was to appreciate and then value the diversity of thought that we brought to every endeavor. Now, in our senior years, these opposing points of view, which we confidently anticipate, give us many moments of mutually enjoyed laughter.

Carol and David's relationship was cemented by the support they gave one another on large issues, including the worst pain imaginable, the loss of a child. Like other couples whom you will meet in this book, shared grief cemented the bond for the Bowies. They also learned flexibility. Carol reflected on the importance of change and said:

During the Decade for Women, David took Women's Studies for his elective courses as he worked, part time over a twelve-year period, to obtain his BA. I audited some of these courses. I would have to say this focus caused the most profound inner restructuring in us and in our relationship. We are quite strong individually and have, over the years, become a very strongly connected couple. We are equally comfortable being together and saying nothing or vigorously exploring whys and whats.

Where did the time go? Growing up and growing together within the framework of our covenant with each other.

Elizabeth Rochester shared some perspectives from her marriage with Michael. She said, "It is a happy one, that is true, and there has been lots of work for both of us to do to make it so, but I doubt that there is anything particularly interesting or significant about the process. It has involved the usual: learning how to consult; learning how to give voice to feelings and struggles which can produce temporary tempests in a teacup, but which also produce deeper understanding and better 'ways' with one another."

She shared the following example:

Let me give you only one wee taste (and Michael should really give one too, but I know he hasn't time, and I doubt that I could do a good job of relating a story from his side). The scene: Michael has just come home and I am in the final stages of making dinner. Timing is of the essence, if everything is going to reach the table, hot. He immediately starts washing dishes in the sink, which puts him in my way, big time. I ask him to do something else which would be helpful, but not in the way, "I can't; I'm busy doing . . ." I say nothing, but I am tense and irritated.

Later, I realize that, while I appreciate his eagerness to be helpful and "understand" that his motivation is 100%, in fact, over the years, there has been a growing tension and sense of resentment. Why had I not consulted with him about it? For after all, we consulted about a lot of things. The reason was because I also knew that it felt trivial to me, that if I tried to talk about it, it would seem that I had no sense of appreciation for a man whom many women would find positively angelic. I also knew that he would feel hurt, even angry at not being appreciated, and "things would be worse" for a time, and nothing much might change. It didn't feel worth the risk. But, I also knew that a lack of frankness can lead to alienation, and the building tension was a warning sign.

The next morning, I sat myself down and tried to figure out how to give voice to my view. I prayed about it. I remembered the guidance of 'Abdu'l-Bahá, from *Selections from the Writings of 'Abdu'l-Bahá*: "training the girl children; . . . the cultivation of a good character, . . . perseverance, strength, determination, firmness of purpose; with household management."[3] Aha! Household management. Managers direct the services of employees. Right! I wrote to Michael, saying I wonder how he would feel if I went into his office and began tidying up his papers, without asking him. Then I explained that the time pressures, just before dinner is served, are not caused by my starting dinner late but caused by the need to have everything finish cooking at the same time. During that period of time, I do not need someone between me and the sink, between me and the counter. I need to let you know what would be helpful.

Now, of course, I don't have a copy of the letter I wrote, so that is only a rough idea of what I wrote. What I do remember is that he read the letter, looked up at me and said, "That makes perfect sense." And from then on, he came into the kitchen and asked what he could do to help. I really appreciate the fact that he has such a strong hold on the principle of equality, that it doesn't bother him to take direction from me, or me from him.

The only reason I dare tell such a trivial story is that I know that trivialities can build up and, like a pressure cooker, blow up at most unexpected times and in very messy ways. That has happened too, and more than once.

I found this story very useful. First, it offered another way of consulting—through a letter—that, as a writer, I found helpful. This method of consulting had the obviously positive element of having to gather one's thoughts, edit them, and not have an immediate and possibly emotional response. It was very practical. Also, it was grounded in research from the Bahá'í writings, where the writings were applied to an everyday living situation. Additionally, Elizabeth's story reinforced my own feeling that it is best not to let small challenges build up into bigger ones but to deal with them quietly, calmly, and lovingly as they arise. Finally, I was impressed that while in one situation a satisfactory response could come forth, there was acknowledgment that sometimes, one is simply not going to be able to be so reasonable, and that marriage can survive, endure, and grow happily through the process of resolving conflicts, small and large. What was needed was respect and patience.

Patience

David Brown and his wife Haodan, married for far less time, agreed with the need for patience in a different context. David said,

> If one is patient and detached before marriage, thoroughly investigates and chooses wisely for marriage, and then accepts and nurtures in marriage, then one's marriage will be a source of immense happiness, comfort and enjoyment. It is one of the most important decisions of your life because it will affect the rest of your entire life. It is my belief that if a person is patient, open, and selfless enough, God will eventually arrange the opportunity to meet a person that is right for him or her because marriage is a law of God. I had to travel all the way to China, but eventually I met a person that was right for me and am now much happier. I wish this happiness for everyone.

Happy marriages evolve over time. David and Haodan, unlike most of those who have given their perspectives from marriage, have just begun their journey. This is in contrast with the Schuurmans, who have been married for half a century.

Suzanne and Hubert Schuurman had chosen the Bahá'í Faith as young adults, and their story also crosses cultures. Of Polish and Danish descent, respectively, Suzanne and Hubert had left Europe in the wake of the Second World War. Suzanne observed that one should not enter a marriage expecting the spouse to change, and she offered her perspective on how she had approached marriage:

Before I married, my mother advised me not to expect my husband to change. She suggested that I multiply all the faults I know of by ten; if I still felt I could live with him—to go ahead. Looking back on life, that was good advice. Shared spiritual goals are important though one comes to realize that love for Bahá'u'lláh expresses itself in many ways. Overlook the faults of others, and "One must see in every human being only that which is worthy of praise" are helpful mottos. One of the qualities that I very much appreciate in Hubert is that he does not find fault with me and is easy to please, appreciative and supportive.

Suzanne spoke further to some of the things which can undermine a marriage: "The greatest test to a marriage can be little annoyances, habits that can be a constant irritation. These may not bring a marriage to the edge of dissolution but can increase tension to a dangerous degree. The solution I have worked out for these is to practice the 'sin-covering eye' by imagining a net (mine is a deep midnight-blue) studded with star-like brilliants that represent my spouse's sterling qualities.[4] This net I throw, in my mind's eye, over the annoyances. They then appear like a night sky dotted with stars."

Suzanne noted, however, that there is an element of personal responsibility in the development of a marital relationship, as did several of the other contributors. Both partners needed to have a willingness to demonstrate an ownership of their own feelings, rather than attributing an inappropriate emotional response to someone else's faults. Both husband and wife needed a desire to avoid blaming, in order to understand what was really going on in connection with another human soul.

Suzanne added, "A marriage pitfall that I often fall into is of my own making. It consists of the formula, 'If he loves me then he would . . .' I have stumbled and fallen into countless such traps of my own devising. Let me give you an example. It is our tenth wedding anniversary, but my dear husband does not seem to have remembered. My mind complains, 'I shouldn't need to remind him, if he loved me he would . . .' But that year he is preoccupied and does not remember. I weep silently and my resentment grows until we are both tripping over it. Finally it all comes out and we make up. Contritely he takes me out to supper and a while later buys a lovely gift."

It occurred to me, while reading this account, that one aspect of sustained marriage must be the ability to acknowledge another's feelings and to make an apology. Suzanne, however, pointed out the importance of recognizing that it is not Hubert's job to read her mind or to fulfill her expectations, and that she herself could take action to remedy the situation as described:

Since then I have learned to lead up to anniversaries ahead of time and engage in consultation. One year I even planned my own birthday party with a magician, live entertainment, and dozens of friends. The resentment trap is ever ready to trip one up, and it does not seem to be something that I have been able to avoid once and for all. For many years I have fallen into its manifold variations. After one particularly painful episode I was praying when a sudden realization came like an illumination. If I had had one of those rare, totally enveloping love relationships (if any such actually exist), would I have been drawn to rely on prayer and develop the relationship with God that trials and tests have led me to do?

In other words, if marriage were perfect, there would be no need to grow! Suzanne continued,

Tests come in all forms and at all times. When I was young I thought that after twenty years of marriage all the kinks would have been worked out. But I was in my mid-50s when I overheard my husband talking about our marriage to a young friend whose own marriage was about to end. I was in the kitchen, and they were in the dining room when I heard my husband describe our marriage in terms of an easy compatibility and many shared interests—nothing derogatory, just the opposite—yet I was so staggered that I had to go out of the house and wander around in a daze until tired. I found sanctuary in a chapel where I could sit and think.

I had lived with my husband for over twenty-five years, and yet I did not recognize the marriage he described. How could we share the same house and the same bed, travel to the same places, and yet not share the same reality? I was flabbergasted, stunned, and unbelieving. Yet I had heard him describe a marriage that worked effortlessly, whereas I saw it as a work in progress requiring constant effort and much sacrifice. This episode came only a few years after (our son) Tristan's death, and I was still recovering from the difference

in grief between men and women, our move to a new local-
ity, the sacrifice of a teaching job I had loved. My perception
of marriage was more of a deeply plowed field than a meadow
of flowers. This experience left me with the indelible realization of how different is each person's reality.

Like the Schuurmans, who have been married for almost
fifty years, Bea and Clyde MacTavish stressed the value of
patience. Bea mentioned, among other things, how much
she admired her husband's patience. Clyde and Bea
MacTavish are originally from Nova Scotia, but when I met
them it was because Bea had become a Bahá'í in their new
home in Western Quebec. Her husband, Clyde, was the principal of my high school. Now retired, both Bea and Clyde
have been battling with health issues but welcome visitors,
and I have enjoyed their kind hospitality. On this occasion,
we reminisced a little, and then I told them about my book.

"How many years have you been married?" I asked.

"Forty-nine," answered Clyde.

It turned out that they shared the same wedding anniversary as my husband and I, December 21, and that on December 21, 2007, they will celebrate their fiftieth anniversary. I asked if they were looking forward to it, but Clyde
seemed noncommittal.

Bea said of Clyde, "Everything's 'God willing.' Clyde got
that from his Scottish grandmother."

My grandmother had used that expression a lot, as well. I
asked Clyde if he could remember what it was that had attracted him to Bea.

He smiled and said, "I can't remember that far back." Then
he paused and added, "Actually, it's true that the older you

get, the easier it is to remember things from longer ago than it is to remember the more recent events."

I asked Bea what had attracted her to Clyde, whom she affectionately calls "Bucky." Her answer surprised me. She said, "It was a blind date."

I had never previously encountered anyone who had actually married someone **they** met on a blind date, and she told the story:

> My co-worker, also a public health nurse, phoned to ask if I would go out with her boyfriend's friend. I told her that I didn't go on blind dates, but finally relented, and the strangest thing happened. They came to pick me up and as Clyde came through the door I heard a voice say, "This is the man you will marry." It was startling, but I said nothing at the time and put it out of mind. One of the things that attracted me to Clyde is that he read *Time* magazine. Well, I thought, this is great, he will know what is going in the world and I will learn a lot from him. And I have! Clyde has a wonderful sense of humor and his wit is legendary. Not a day goes by when we don't have a laugh or two. He is also very thoughtful—he still surprises me with bouquests of roses and treats from Tim Hortons.

Clyde noted that it would be very difficult to really understand what makes any given marriage work, because there is so much that is only between the couple and that cannot be shared with anyone else. I understood this very well: in any long term relationship, understandings grow which are non-verbal, built on history, familiarity, shared stories, and conversations. Couples can communicate across a room with a single glance, or an event will trigger a memory and they will simultaneously exclaim, "Do you remember?" and then look at one another and know that they are about to tell the same story.

Their mutual affection was clear, based on a deep knowledge of one another's character, the shared events of almost a half-century in one another's company, and the easy companionship which comes from building a family together.

The Bahá'í Faith in Marriage

Karin Ferguson noted that she appreciated the protection that Bahá'í laws offered. Karin and Ian Ferguson were not members of the Bahá'í Faith when they married, and in fact Karin became a Bahá'í a decade into the marriage. While Ian was supportive, he did not join her in her chosen faith for another nine years. She shared the story of their spiritual search: "When we encountered the Bahá'í Faith, we were with the Canadian military. Ian was a jet pilot and flew for the Forces for twenty-five years. Service life was *not* conducive to spiritual questing, believe me, but I had been a seeker since I was very young, wanting to find truth in religion. Did God have a plan for mankind? And did He have one for me, personally?"

Karin's description of her process, and Ian's, is not unlike many of the stories of how people find a new religion while married. She said, "Ian was not seeking at the time and only started coming out to meetings when I told him, 'Fair is fair! You want me to come to events at the Officer's Mess . . . then you come and find out what I'm teaching the children about the Bahá'í Faith!' He was mostly always supportive of what I did with the children. Ian also cashed in his Life Insurance Policy in 1972, so I could go on pilgrimage to Israel."

Karin's involvement with her new faith, and her teaching the children what she believed, was important to the Fergusons. She said,

I know that the writings of the Bahá'í Faith had a profound effect upon Ian, and he became a Bahá'í nine years after me. I really do think that our source of unity, to begin with, was the fact that both of us came from very similar homes—similar in background, similar in our upraising. His parents were wonderful, and so were mine. Although neither set of our parents was very religious, yet their standards and morals were very high and they taught their children the same way.

We have seen so many marriages with horrendous problems over the years. We see marriages affected by the ravages of alcohol—and of course that increases the possibility of spousal abuse. We thank God that Bahá'u'lláh has forbidden the drinking of alcohol in the Bahá'í Faith, as obedience to that law is a big protector for the unity in a marriage. We also thank God that through the years we found the healing power in this faith and solidified our goals together in service. We respect each other, encourage each other in our independence, and keep in solid touch with our children, who are many thousands of miles from us.

Have we made mistakes? Absolutely, but we have faced them together with a lot of prayers and consultation which is always a unifying process. We remember how much we love our family and keep encouraging them as much as possible.

Ginny and Greg Kintz stressed the critical importance of consultation to their marriage as well: "Consultation is what makes our marriage. We have developed this as a habit over the years, and now we consult about everything, large and small. One of the practices that has helped us with large decisions . . . is to list the pros and cons of each option. It helps to make the choices more concrete. Prayer is also an important part of our major decision making. We seldom make a major decision without time for prayer first."

Janis Zrudlo noted the importance of humor, consultation, and collaboration:

It seems to me that one of the great keys to successful marriage is that each partner encourages and allows the other to develop intellectually and spiritually. During our marriage, and even with family and children in tow, the two of us (at different times) pursued university degrees and adjusted to family life. . . . I think we both helped each other with our special projects—I know I edited two theses for Leo, and this brings a closeness that is exciting and stimulating. I think we have always enjoyed a certain clash of ideas, a difference of personality and a freedom of expression that is liberating and joyful. As the other accomplishes something, you feel that this is also your accomplishment. We both agree that a sense of humor is definitely *the* most essential part of any successful marriage. Sometimes we just have to look at each other, and we know exactly what was funny without saying anything.

Fortunately, we have been blessed with very similar creative and artistic tastes, and these things have also given us great comfort and joy—especially with all the trials and tests one faces and cannot avoid in life. I am so glad that I married an architect—I think I would have otherwise been a hopeless wife of an astrophysicist—and I know Leo appreciates that fact that I had a musical background, as we both love and pursue all activities related to these fields of endeavor. There is so much to share and talk about!

Then, of course, there is our faith, which is the greatest joy of all in our lives. Here our creative energies can really soar, and our helpmate in life becomes essential in all that we wish for ourselves, and for others. To not feel that you are helpless and adrift in life, but to feel that you are actually participating in and building for the future—why, this is the very cement that establishes and solidifies for all time that marriage is indeed "a fortress for well-being."[5] And for this we are truly grateful.

Respect

Another couple spoke considerably about the role of culture in maintaining their happy marriage. They felt that their love was conflated with respect. Gillian and Parviz Mottahed are a couple where the husband is a somewhat traditional Iranian. They, too, shared some of their perspectives on the various challenges they had faced. In particular, I asked the Mottaheds how they deal with it when they are angry with one another.

Gillian said, "The big word is RESPECT. Whether or not you go along with the viewpoint of the other's culture, you have to accept and not criticize, because ideas of what is normal and what isn't can run very deep in different cultures."

Parviz agrees, to a degree. "You do accept, but there is a last ten percent of cultural difference that is designated, as one could say, 'no-go,' but the other person must accept this difference unconditionally. There is no choice really: either one is going to allow this room or oppose it."

He added that it had been very important that Gillian had spent time in Iran. "Gillian had the opportunity to come to Iran and see how my people lived."

Gillian added, "Otherwise it would be very difficult. Adjusting to the Persian culture is very hard: you have to address different people different ways. This may sound strange to the Western culture. One respects and accepts the tradition, and no questions are asked. There is no room for dissent. The respect level is very high."

I asked them how they solved problems when dissent did, in fact, arise.

Gillian: "With the move back to the U.K., and now to Canada, the conditions and the environment are totally different. It's a different ballgame. You agree to differ in many ways, and life goes on. This is a systematic and continuous process. It is not possible to solve everything, but one works on it and smoothes it out as one goes along. We haven't solved everything."

I asked, "Did one of you yield?"

They replied simultaneously, "Yes!"

Parviz surprised me and said, "I did, by letting go of some of my 'Persian-ness.'"

Gillian agreed and added, "Because we were living in the West."

Parviz illustrated his attitude with a story. "Difficulties and problems arise but have to be solved one way or the other. My grandmother, who lived to be about a hundred, told me about a wise man, who, when asked why he didn't get angry or bothered, said, 'All troubles are like one hair. I am at one end and the world is at the other. When you pull out that hair, I'm on one end, and the others are pulling. I let go.' So, I let go in some ways of doing things."

Another couple, Pat and Sandy Slobodian, shared the following summary of their observations: "We met over a Ping-Pong table in grade eleven, and since that time we have walked the same path. We married at the age of eighteen, and after over thirty years of marriage are mindful of the true value inherent in a spiritual union. We offer these gleanings in the hope that others may find them useful."

The Slobodians suggested the following ideas: strive for an intimate communion but cultivate a respectful detachment, maintain a dynamic relationship between attending to self and to the rights of the other, and foster an attitude of independence from all (save God) while employing the power of the marital bond.

I noted, in their list, that the familiar word *respect*—and also the word *independence*—had appeared. They further suggested the following: educate oneself in the ways and use of playfulness and dependability, and learn together how to rely on prayer as well as how to find practical solutions to life's problems.

Here again, as with other couples, there is a balance between fun and commitment. I noted the use of prayer coupled with practicality!

Pat and Sandy also gave this advice: commit to being as courteous to one another as one would be to a friend or acquaintance, fight one's own spiritual battles, and be compassionately mindful of one another's trials.

To risk a tautology, the process of marriage is a process. Couples indicated that they needed to develop particular attitudes as they lived with their loved one. Susan Eghrari Moraes put her thoughts this way:

> Marriage is a continuous, developing process, and we have to take advantage of this process. My husband and I have different backgrounds. We are both Brazilians. Tunico, short for Antonio, comes from a typical Brazilian family from the south of Brazil. He is a descendant of Portuguese, Italian, Spanish, German, and native Indians. The concepts of family, tradition, education, and a good character are very strong in his family. My parents came from Iran to Brazil as Bahá'í pioneers in the mid-50s. We descend from Persian Jews. The concepts of family, perseverance, good character, and education are important issues from my side. The process of marriage—from both sides of our family—has different implications from the model based on a consumer society. The consumer society wants to drag out whatever it can from the situation because it is an egotistical method to get to one's goal. This model teaches couples to not care about the future or the consequences of their actions. There is a need to exchange this view for one that looks at marriage as a relationship that is sustainable, recognizes it as a dynamic process, and teaches married couples to care about their future together.

The first years of our marriage were a continuous adaptation to the new model. My thoughts and actions had a great influence from the consumer society. I would see myself in the context of the present time, and if I have given so much of myself to the marriage, what benefits would I gain?

Susan noted that a particular quotation impacted her thinking. The quotation read, "They are two helpmates, two intimate friends, who should be concerned about the welfare of each other."[6] This quote made her reflect on a different way of looking at marriage:

"Concerned about the welfare of each other" is a precious key. My husband and I work together; we are both architects. We have some clients in common and others not, but we see each other a good part of the day. We have been married for over twenty years. Every evening, I ask him, how was his day. Sometimes I tell him about my day. There always has to be a channel open between husband and wife. This communication channel can be verbal or written, or it can be a look, a smile, a touch. Sometimes, to communicate meaningfully is simply to listen with attention. Whenever I ask my husband how his day went, most of the time, his answers are simply "it was good," and he leaves it at that. But the point is that the channel is open, and every once in a while he surprises me by telling me about an incident or asking my opinion about an issue related to what happened to him that day.

An interesting theme that emerged from the various accounts of marriage was that although marriage was a joining of spirits, it was also a journey full of expectations, and that some of those views had, inevitably, to change with the day-to-day reality of living with another person. One writer, Edna Nablo, commented on what she thought was a somewhat facile approach to marriage, one that undermined the possibility of its longevity. She said,

> It is reported that 'Abdu'l-Bahá said, "Lay the foundation of your affection in the very center of your spiritual being, at the very heart of your consciousness, and let it not be shaken by adverse winds."[7] When two people follow this guidance, in a very real sense the two of you become one, so that when anything is being considered it is "we" who are considering, rather than one of the "Is" in the partnership. My simplistic perception of why many of today's marriages fail is that they do not seem to accomplish this, and so they become competitors within the marriage, rather than loving cooperators. No doubt the Hollywood-created expectations about marriage is that it is a continual fulfillment of romantic love, not requiring the participants to do much more than look pretty and be there to have their dreams fulfilled. Our culture also does not address the reality that marriage is a sacred institution whose purpose is to serve a vital role in society. It is not mere gratification for the marriage partners. If romantic and sexual gratification are present in a marriage, that's like icing on the cake, but it does not mean that the marriage has failed if they are not present.

Sacrifice

According to the couples I interviewed, a central concept of a successful marriage is the idea that marriage is not meant, necessarily, to be a fulfillment of romantic love. Successful marriages are more than "looking pretty" and "fulfilling dreams." In fact, one of the themes that emerged in almost every narrative was a necessity for one spouse to sacrifice for the other. To do this without resentment, with an appreciation of the differences in the other, seems to be an intimate spiritual connection, rather than an impelling physical one. The connection of spirit is apparently very important to people who honor, still, the "sacrament" of marriage. Several others noted that this spiritual connection had been foundational to the success of their marriage.

Rick Gordon, married to Nahid, who is Iranian, for thirty-six years, observed,

Seeing someone else sacrifice for another has a profound impact on my feelings. Making our marriage work was harder earlier on when the added responsibilities of raising children and developing work skills diverted our attention. As we moved past those challenges, we were able to focus more energy on our relationship, and the stresses diminished. As this continued, we were able to enjoy each other's company more. I also became less analytical and precise in my attempts to solve problems, and I let things ride more often, allowing outside distractions to defuse difficult situations. Shifting the emphasis from independent community service more towards strengthening the family also made a significant improvement in our relationship with each other and with community members.

Edward Epp, married to his wife Leanne for over a quarter century, shared the following:

> If I were to speak generally about what is most valuable to make a marriage work—to enable the maximum positive, in happiness, longevity, and health—if compelled to simplify it to the most basic concept, I would have to state that adherence to a spiritual discipline is the most important factor. For me, and for Leanne too, I am sure, the moderating influence of the Bahá'í teachings—the Bahá'í spirit, stories, models, community service, and prayers—have again and again countered the forces that would tear the relationship apart: distractions, illusions, even seemingly persuasive arguments that might otherwise prevent the relationship from gradually growing to a mature, stable, calm level where we can more easily be convinced of the value of this marriage and of sticking it out. It ain't easy, but it is usually worth it!

Peter Brady talked about the enduring nature of marriage and said,

> It was not easy, and it still is not easy. But it is worth the effort we have made. Often I think that my wife has made more efforts than I have. It has never been impossible, nor a great burden. We love each other and see whatever tests come our way as challenges to be faced and overcome. They are not seen as reasons to consider separation or di-

vorce. . . . Most often it is my wife who accepts and endures tests with a more cheerful attitude.

The work of keeping our marriage alive is not an arduous task or burden; it is a joy and privilege to be together. Any effort we make is not perceived as work or obligation in any negative sense. What we do comes from the commitment we made because we know it is necessary and, above all, because we choose to do it out of love.

Vitality in a Marriage

The emergence into a new phase, a rebirth, is the reward for many couples who persevere. I suspect that one element of this process may be keeping a sense of humor. Marilyn Smith's perspective, like Janis Zrudlo's, emphasized the importance of humor. She said, "Our marriage and its health and vitality have been a shared goal and a priority to us . . . We wanted our children to grow up in a happy, moral, and united home and in an environment where faith became the center of their lives, too. We really enjoy being together, working together, and serving together. Laughter has been part of our life together."

To my second question—"Are there spiritual principles or values which you feel have been particularly useful or of assistance in your success in marriage?"—Marilyn answered, "Loyalty, faithfulness, sacrifice, unity, tolerance, sense of humor, forgiveness, patience, trustworthiness, courtesy, service. Without these principles and values, it would be difficult to have a happy marriage."

June Barrow, answering the same question, conveyed the same idea: "Honesty and a desire to be of service to our faith and to others have been the most important values, but there are also many others. When we consult or try to find answers to problems, we ask, what is the spiritual principle involved?"

Marilee Rhody said, "We are conscious of the fact that we are the eternal spiritual helpmates of one another."

Sylvia de Vasquez noted, "I needed to know that my husband's commitment was to something higher than me in a way that would not cause conflict with my commitment to something higher. Marrying someone of a different faith, with the same values as my own, would not have worked for me. . . . I particularly could not have handled being married to someone convinced I was going to hell. 'I love you but I'm afraid for your soul' would not have worked for me."

Bahá'ís are not discouraged from marrying people of other beliefs, but Sylvia clearly felt that such an approach would not have worked for her.

She added, "Regarding 'activity' in faith—that's an individual couple thing. Yovanny's service to his faith, at the moment, is in the financial and spiritual support of his family, and I honor that as extremely valid."

Sylvia adds an interesting note, regarding cultural differences and how they impacted their marriage: "From a mixing-of-cultures point of view, it is interesting, but while Yovanny and I both feel that you have to be very cautious when wanting to marry someone of a different culture, the mixing of our cultures has not provided any serious challenges to our marriage; if anything, it has allowed us to complement each other."

Sylvia and Yovanny have spent most of their marriage, including the birth of their three children, in Belize. They have now relocated to Canada, and I will be interested in finding out from them, as time goes on, whether their cultural differences come more into play in a different nation, where her husband is more in the minority. For the time being, her letters regarding their adjustments note only that they are ready for a Canadian winter and that so far, the only aspect of Canadian life that Yovanny does not enjoy is "static electricity."

For this couple, their shared spiritual beliefs contribute to a daily working relationship of respect and love.

This view is confirmed by Ho-San and Mariette Leong. Ho-San is Chinese and his wife, Mariette, is Australian. I met them in the late 1970s, in Papua New Guinea, when we were all Bahá'í pioneers there. Their children were small then. Here is a little of their story, as Ho-San shared it: "Mariette and I have been married for over thirty-five years. We celebrated this on the 27th of December, 2004, with a short holiday break up the coast, about two hours from where we live. It sounds like a lifetime; the years have come and gone, and today we can look back with lots of pleasant memories of bringing up a family of five—four of our own and Seff, our precious adopted daughter from our pioneering days in Papua New Guinea. She is regarded as the eldest of her siblings ever since she joined us way back in April 1975."

Ho-San shared this metaphor:

I like to believe that our marriage is made of earth and heaven, in the rich Chinese traditions that emphasize the importance of the family as an integral part of the community and the society we live in. Mariette teases me sometimes, saying that the longer she is married to me, the more she realizes what a "Chinaman" I am! However, at the end of the day, it really does not matter that I am Chinese and that she is quintessentially Australian. What has mattered is that we make of it what we are prepared to put into it. Over the years I tell her that no matter what, we must always try to keep the candle burning, even though at times it seemed like the flame would disappear as we struggled to keep our bodies and souls together.

Mariette's father, Collis Featherstone, was a distinguished teacher of the Bahá'í Faith. Ho-San remembered his influence: "We have a long-standing joke we share with each other and the children, borrowed from her wonderful, precious father. He used to say of his dearly beloved wife that she was the best wife he ever had! So, when the going gets somewhat rough and even when it gets easy enough, I tease her with this same line spoken by her dad, and we then laugh about it, and make fun of each other. It's a wonderful way to release tensions and difficulties."

I asked how the passing of time had affected their marriage.

Ho-San replied, "Age has not dimmed the love we have for each other. Yes, we have grown much older now, but like autumn, the season of mists and mellow fruitfulness, our marriage has definitely become fruitful and rich with variety and experience. And, most of all, it has enabled us to render services, as undeserving and humble as they are, in the Faith of Bahá'u'lláh in all these years of our married life, both in Australia and Papua New Guinea."

Summarizing, Ho-San said,

> I don't know that there is a magic formula for an ideally successful marriage. It is a lot of hard work, tears, and sweat thrown into the bargain, but out of it has come joy and blessings beyond measure. We seem to have grown into each other's lives, separate but also together. Whenever I think of this it gives me much happiness. So, Heather, I don't know what else to add, there is much to write, yet it is hard to express in the confinement of words. The heart knows, and that really is all that matters. Two people from different cultures, and different parts of the world, come together and make their marriage a declaration of their love for each other, on earth and in heaven!

Mariette added to her husband's thoughts:

> I read Ho-San's account of our marriage this morning. He had written it last night after I had gone to bed. I told him I had one thing to add to it: of all the virtues in marriage, I think listening is one of the most important. If we listen we come to "know," if we listen we come to "understand," if we listen we can "feel," and if we listen we can "hear," and if we listen we can "see," and we need all of these virtues in order to "consult." And most of all we need to listen to our own heart. All of this listening will keep us out of trouble! So that is my addition, for what it is worth!

Religion in Marriage

How does spiritual life affect marriages? These are couples who pray together, who come from differing cultural perspectives, and who, in Sylvia's case, offer the idea that the commitment to God is in some ways higher than the commitment to the partner. The Bahá'í marriage vow articulates precisely this ideal: "We will all, verily, abide by the will of God."

All religious traditions have seen marriage as a unity of souls. This aspect of spirit is much neglected in most modern ideas of what marriage should be, or can be. Marriage should supposedly be based on attraction, mutual goals, and self-fulfillment. All of these aspects may or may not exist in these marriages, in varying degrees, but most of these couples talked of shared service to a higher goal. Their attraction was, and is, spiritual as well as physical or emotional. There are some words of 'Abdu'l-Bahá, who serves as a moral exemplar for Bahá'ís, on the subject of this spiritual attraction: "Each sees in the other the Beauty of God reflected in the soul, and finding this point of similarity, they are attracted to one another in love."[8]

Religious writings do not appear, generally, to emphasize physical attraction. Secular writings tend to emphasize "worldly" goals: financial success, "successful" children, physical health. All of these are acknowledged within these marriages, but they are placed in a larger context, of spirit and service.

Marilyn Smith explained, "We have sought, over the years, the elements for creating unity, pleasing our spouse, serving our Creator, and developing as individuals simultaneously.

Neither our spouse nor our children have been the center of our lives. We have tried to make service to our faith our collective center."

Suzanne Schuurman offered some thoughts on marriages grounded in a faithful spirit: "Marriage is a relationship and institution of such mystery! I like to think of it as an expression of the same uniting principle that holds molecules and atoms together, that keeps planets in their orbits, and that anchors us down to earth through gravity. Love is a magnet—a basic ingredient of a universal binding force."

She noted that her religious background had affected her definition of spiritual life:

The Catholicism of my childhood provided a mixed message about woman: Eve the temptress led us into original sin, yet the Virgin Mary was unblemished in her holiness. Everyday women were either nuns who renounce their femininity to become "brides of Christ," or wives and mothers with no say as to the size of their family. In paintings (my mother was a great believer in taking her daughter to art galleries), I noticed that the female form—clothed and unclothed—was beloved by artists. It was through the arts that I developed a sense of womanhood, but it is in the Bahá'í writings that I discovered a legitimization of the love experience, for finding and coming to love the Manifestation of God is compared to that magical, transforming experience of "falling in love."

There were no models of successful marriages around me as I grew up. My father had died in a yachting accident when I was four, so I did not have the example of my immediate family. In my Polish environment, infidelity was accepted on the part of men, though not condoned in women. I didn't know Canadian marriages well enough to assess them . . . It was only through reading that I came to form a picture of romantic love and marriage. The story of Layli and Majnun* and other tragic tales appealed to my young imagination. Somewhere in my childhood the conviction that marriage was meant to last must have lodged in my heart and mind.

As Suzanne commented, she had "discovered a legitimization of the love experience." She called "falling in love" an experience that is "magical, transforming" and added, "marriage was meant to last." This leads us to the next foundational concept for successful marriages: love.

---

* The story of Layli and Majnun is a Middle Eastern love story, and it is somewhat similar to the Western story of Romeo and Juliet.

2

LOVE

Love suffereth long, and is kind; love envieth not;
love vaunteth not itself, is not puffed up, doth not behave
itself unseemly, seeketh not its own, is not provoked,
taketh not account of evil; rejoiceth not in
unrighteousness, but rejoiceth with the truth;
beareth all things; believeth all things, hopeth
all things, endureth all things. Love never faileth:
but whether there be prophecies, they shall be done
away; whether there be tongues, they shall cease;
whether there be knowledge, it shall be done away.
For we know in part, and we prophesy in part;
but when that which is perfect is come, that which
is in part shall be done away. When I was as a child,
I spake as a child, I felt as a child, I thought as a child:
now that I am become a man, I have put away
childish things. For now we see in a mirror, darkly;
but then face to face: now I know in part;
but then shall I know fully even as also I was
fully known. But now abideth faith,
hope, love, these three; and the greatest of these is love.

1 Corinthians 13:1–13

Probably the most essential ingredient for any marriage is love. Not surprisingly, however, each of the individuals interviewed for this book had a different idea for defining what is meant by "love." I asked each of the couples to tell how love had shaped their marriage. Here are these parts of the stories.

Love as Fate

One of the sweetest love stories in this book came from an extraordinary couple. Hélène Wallingford Panalaks and Dr. Thavil Panalaks, known to his friends as Tony, were married more than forty-five years ago. Their love story is an uncommon one and spans many years, highlighted by their travels together. In serving together all over the globe, their love grew at every level, as Hélène explained. Tony is from Thailand and is of Buddhist background; Hélène is a French-Canadian, born a Roman Catholic. Tony's notes to me read as follows: "Thavil (Tony) Panalaks was born in Bangkok on November 9th, 1917 and educated in Bangkok and Padhumthani. He left home in then Siam on June 3, 1938, on a cargo ship . . . and arrived in Hawaii with hardly any money in his pocket. He worked his way through school as a houseboy and graduated from McKinley High School and later from the University of Hawaii in 1943."

The biography continued, citing Tony's movement to Cornell University in Ithaca, New York, and later to Toronto and then Ottawa, Ontario, Canada, where he was to meet his wife. During his time in New York, Tony met Bahá'ís, and although he did not spend time investigating this faith, he became "reacquainted with Bahá'í students" when he arrived in Toronto, for further studies. In 1957, Tony declared himself to be a Bahá'í. He also met Hélène Wallingford, and they were married shortly thereafter. Ten years went by, and in 1967, Hélène, too, became a Bahá'í.

Hélène wrote, "We did not have any children of our own but had nine students, Thai, who were nieces and nephews, sons and daughters of Tony's Thai relatives and friends, who were sponsored for many years in Gatineau."

The Panalaks make their home in Gatineau, Québec, across the Ottawa River from the capital city of Canada. Hélène continued, "Most of the Thai nieces and nephews were of the Buddhist faith; one nephew was of the religion of Islam. We never had discussions of their religions. I was then of the Catholic faith and my mother also, and my father was of the Protestant faith. He did not meet these students, as he had died before their coming."

Hélène continued the story of each of these children, who are very dear to her and to Tony. Hélène also noted her pride in Tony's many accomplishments (his Curriculum Vitae is very lengthy with the various honors he has received in his professional pursuits.) Hélène, too, has been honored for her significant contributions to her profession, in public health.

Hélène noted, "In every country visited, I try to meet the public health nurses, showing them my love and appreciation; also, we made it a point to connect with and meet the Bahá'ís in every country visited."

She added, "My aim was to have the French and English nurses to get to know each other and to break barriers in prejudices—for example, between different religions and languages. I also wanted to teach more advanced techniques, and more importantly, to get to be respectful of other religions, races, and people."

Tony's biography, written a few years ago, lists the many countries they have visited, as follows: "During their forty years together, they have traveled around the world visiting Bahá'í friends in thirty-two countries including (besides

Thailand), Pakistan, Vietnam, India, Laos, Nepal, Malaysia, Israel, Singapore, Panama, Indonesia, Costa Rica, Hong Kong, Spain, Japan, Gibraltar, Hawaii, Iran, Germany, Bali."

This is what Hélène wrote about their marriage:

> We have been married, Tony and I, for forty-five years last September, 2004. It has been a time of growth, of getting to know each other, to appreciate each other, to grow in maturity, to be united in love, to keep our personality.
>
> We passed through periods of growth—from love at first sight to knowing what it means to love. We gradually gained maturity and a depth of appreciation for each other, and we were able to more fully understand one another, to forgive each other, and to pray together. We learned to accept each other's diverse qualities, such as our race and our former religious beliefs. We also learned to respect one another's ideas, even if we held different viewpoints about something. During these forty-five years of marriage, I personally have grown to realize more about love and its meaning, to become more and more responsible for my actions, and to control and improve my character. I have realized that love is eternal.

In telling the story of the fate that led them to one another, Hélène and Tony used the metaphor of chemistry, which seems apt since Tony is a prominent chemist. Tony and Hélène have spent their lives serving their faith. In doing so, they have watched the love they have for one another grow and mature. Of their marriage, they say this: "Tony's relentless life journey may be summarized as a chain of human reactions. . . . First, if Tony had not met the late Chareon Wathan in Bangkok some sixty years ago, he would not have been able to go to Hawaii. Mr. Wathan was the one who helped him to leave Thailand, and if Tony had not met him, he would not have been able to go to Cornell. Also, if Tony had not come to Ottawa, he would not have met Hélène Wallingford, married her over forty years ago, and lived happily together to this day."

Hélène added, "We have come from different parts of this world of ours, and East meets West. We certainly fooled Rudyard Kipling. The twain did meet!" Tony and Hélène served together happily until Tony's death in early 2006. Hélène, when I last spoke with her, was trying to come to terms with how much she misses him.

Falling in Love

Gillian and Parviz Mottahed "fell in love." Yet they were among the couples who emphasized that cross-cultural differences can be very challenging. They have been married for over forty years. They met in England; Parviz is an Iranian, who went to Britain to study mining engineering. Gillian worked in the registrar's office at the University in Leeds. She was not quite nineteen when she went to a dance on campus. Bored, she was about to leave when Parviz arrived with some friends. He asked her to dance. I asked her if she believed that this was "destiny." She answered, definitely, in the affirmative.

Gillian is a very soft-spoken woman, while Parviz is outgoing and boisterous. He was very different from anyone she'd met: in those days, there were few "foreigners" in the area and even fewer from the Middle East. Yet Gillian felt what she called an "affinity" for people of other cultures. I asked her, "Did you fall in love?"

"Oh, yes," she exclaimed. I asked her to define that.

"To me, it meant I couldn't imagine my life if he weren't in it. I didn't like it when I didn't see him. That's still true. I don't like it when he goes away. I still have that feeling."

I asked how she knew she wanted to marry him.

"When you love someone like that you want to be with him forever. It's a natural progression."

She added, "In that generation, you didn't live together. You met, fell in love, and got married. It was as simple as that."

She spoke, also, about the theme of commitment. "I think there was total commitment in those days. You didn't look for options or ways out: maybe that's naïve, but I'm glad I didn't have to make the same choices that people have to make today. I'm glad I was brought up in the '60s—I'm not saying people didn't do weird things in the '60s, but my friends and I went through the same process: we met someone, we fell in love, and we married that person."

She spoke about some of the reasons she believes their marriage has been so solid.

"Because my parents were divorced, I wanted to keep a more cohesive family together. I didn't want divorce to happen in my own life, and that may have been a contributing factor to the

'glue' keeping the family together. I don't think this was necessarily a conscious effort on my part, but it could have had something to do with the choices I made—I'm not ruling it out."

I asked her about their religious differences; she was not a
Bahá'í at the time she met Parviz. She said that she decided
to become a Bahá'í on her own, after hearing about the Faith.

She noted, "I was worried, when I wanted to be a Bahá'í,
that people would think it was because I had a Middle Eastern boyfriend, which was unusual, and that he had tried to
convert me. So I waited until Parviz went to Iran for the
summer before I chose to become a Bahá'í. I became a Bahá'í
on my own, and I didn't want anyone to read things into it.
I am able to be very independent."

Love as a Spiritual Duty

Love was also centered in spirituality for Ali Khajavi, who
spoke of the way he had come to care for his wife, Tracy. Ali
had been raised a Muslim in Iran, and he had a very strong
opinion on the importance of his faith to his choice of a
wife. He said, about their different ways of seeing marriage:
"I love her, but it is in a different way than what is popular-
ized in our culture. I love her through Bahá'u'lláh."

I wasn't sure that I understood what he meant by this, and
I asked him to elaborate.

"I love her, as family, as duty, as responsibility."

Still puzzled, I asked him to explain further what he meant.

He said, "I don't have family here. Usually, they would
have suggested someone. When I met Tracy, it was through

our faith. I found her spiritual and kind. She was coming back from service in the Holy Land, in Israel. She could have been tall, short, it didn't matter: I said, that's going to be a perfect marriage."

"Is it?" I asked.

"Through our faith, I am learning how to go as far as possible in a successful marriage."

"So it's not personal," I suggested.

"No," Ali said.

"Does she want it to be personal?" I asked.

"Yes. I think she would like it to be more personal, but I see it as more of a spiritual duty because in this way I can love my wife more."

He continued, "After all, love is about giving with no expectations. When I talk about spirituality, I mean God's love is about giving, so that a person who approaches love as a spiritual duty can be happy with everyone. For me, to have a normal life is to handle situations in a spiritual way."

He explained further, "'Abdu'l-Bahá tells us that when a person has ten qualities, some will be bad and some will be good, and we should concentrate on the good ones because that will increase our love for them. That's what I'm trying to do, to see in her 'maximum qualities.'"

I noted, "It's not like Hollywood."

"No, no," Ali answered, "the kind of love shown in Hollywood movies doesn't exist. It's conditional, and conditional love won't work. This is because all of us are imperfect, and sometimes we are unable to fulfill the conditions upon which conditional love is based. When we're unable to fulfill those conditions, we'll be the first to be disappointed."

He added, "I had expectations regarding Tracy, but the spiritual process is to try and see perfection. A wife and husband should be united inside the home in order to deal with the problems coming from outside. The cause of many separations in marriage is material, especially in the West."

Ali Khajavi had recently been to a talk by Alí Nakhjavání, a respected member of the Bahá'í faith. Mr. Nakhjavání described love as being like a flower that grows stronger as its roots are strengthened and its leaves and blossoms turn towards the sun and rain.

Love as a Progression

Nahid Gordon, also from Iran, offered the following perspective on love: "To me, love is more important than falling in love. Love can be learned and experienced in stages of progression rather than the high expectations of romantically falling in love. When the flame is gone, the coolness will appear. If the base of love is built on unity, it has more chance of surviving."

Nahid's husband Rick added,

When I was young and knew relatively few people well, I thought that I knew what love meant. After having bounced my theories off of others in more recent years, I am far less certain that someone else shares my thoughts when using this term. I link "falling in love" with the chemical "high" experienced in the brain when the body anticipates the growing potential for finding a mate and having offspring. This perception may fail in the romantic polls, but it has been wildly successful at populating the planet. I was "head over heels" with my wife at the beginning, but now consider her much more as a life partner.

We have been married for almost forty years. I decided that she was "the one for me" because we seemed to constantly come closer to each other as we courted, without any negative surprises along the way. Although we had known about each other for one year before becoming engaged, we truly didn't know each other's character well. "Love is blind" is not just a saying.

Nahid added, "Because of two different cultures and upbringings, I had lots of obstacles to overcome. We didn't have much in common either, but we were both willing to serve our faith, which brought the level of understanding and maturity higher than before."

Love and Romance

Another component of love—romance—came from Maury Miloff, who wrote from Bangladesh where he and his wife Helen de Marsh are fulfilling the latest of many international forms of service. He noted that love is essential for a healthy marriage:

I have wrestled, along with most of (Western?) civilization, with middle-age perspectives on marriage, which say something about boredom and seeking a replacement for faded romantic love.

Marriage seems too much down in the trenches most of the time for me to see much inspiration—except when I look back and I see the oceans of love and devotion that surged between us, maintained, preserved, and enhanced us. This love threw on the shores of life three beautiful children, and it nurtured parents, siblings, friends, communities, and ourselves, when we were at our pioneering posts. But it was hard, hard, hard! And times change. Now, we stand on the edge of saying goodbye to all our children, and two of the three of them have already left home. So, the situation has changed and is changing. What will the next phase be? I hope it will be inspiring. I believe it is in our power to make it so.

Maury's wife Helen also viewed marriage in terms of moving through a naive view of romance into a joint spiritual effort grounded in service and family: "I would say that in twenty-five years we have seen well past the illusions of any romantic never-never land that the West still dishes out as a goal of a marriage partnership. I think we have certainly benefited from our efforts to be of service far more than we have, in fact, actually served. Having had our three children—two sons and one daughter—each on his or her own continent, made us heavily reliant on each other and cemented our mutual support system to a degree we might not have felt obliged to achieve."

Maury Miloff and Helen de Marsh both felt that many marriages start out in an idealistic manner but that a shared spiritual purpose had helped develop their own love into something much stronger than a love that is merely based on a naive, romantic wish. Helen noted that our society can negatively affect people's perception of marriage but that, with the proper foundations, marriage can become a sanctuary of peace, stability, and emotional support for the married couple. She said,

All our idealism as young, new Bahá'ís forging a bond together to help rebuild the world got shredded in the reality of the self-destructing world, and we ended up as committed, humbled servants with our foreheads on the threshold of the sacred, terribly grateful just to be alive and together. We have been each other's best friend at the most horrible times, and we have been each other's harshest critic and spared nothing in insisting that the truth prevail. That has pushed us to the limits of our personal resources and forced us to grow.

Being stripped down to the barest essentials—and we are not talking about the fun ones here!—seems to be a devastating experience, a falling into hell of two peoples' imperfections, a going to war and therefore the end of what was a great romance. This tests every notion you had of yourself and your spouse, every fiber of mind, body, and heart, and it is a great way of learning about reality. A ladder of ascension appears, and somehow, slowly, the partners help each other climb out. Hopefully, it works like that if the partners have enough goodness, enough love, enough awareness, enough patience, take enough responsibility . . . and have enough belief that solutions through understanding are possible.

Such honesty can be very painful in a relationship. It is my observation that one needs to feel loved in order to feel comfortable being frank. This seems to be consistent with Helen's view of her marriage with Maury. Together, Helen said, they developed new strengths. She continued,

> We have set ourselves aside to help each other be ful-filled, and we each have stepped back to allow the other to proceed. Anger has been the brilliant red light. It always indicated that boundaries were being overstepped, and we benefited from its glare. That has been a catalyst for us to see the strengths and limitations of the families we came from. The family we have formed is a tremendous source of joy and sustains us just as God does. That people seem to enjoy the company of our children is a wonderful gift, and their growth and struggle to evolve themselves con-tinues to be a wonder. That we are privileged to be confi-dants of our now near-adult children and that we cherish our own relationships with each of them is a benefit I could not have dreamed of.

Here, Helen acknowledged that sometimes, anger has served as a "catalyst" for change. The element of volition, the will to change, assists to control one's own feelings in order to serve the higher purpose of the marriage. This is sometimes facilitated through defusing tensions. Maury brought his irre-pressible sense of humor to his observations: "My last thought on what allowed our marriage to not only survive but func-tion reasonably well: believing that our reality is spiritual, that spirituality is peace, serenity, and bliss, and that it is in our power, and therefore our responsibility, to deal with all situations in a way that we create or enter into that reality. That is the one thing which has most made our marriage work. That, and always getting the other person's permission for damn near everything!"

Marriage as an Everlasting Love Affair

Another couple, Louise Profeit-LeBlanc and her husband Bob, also came from two different cultures and traditions. They met shortly after Louise, an Aboriginal from the Yukon Territory of northern Canada, became a Bahá'í.

They shared what Louise called their "love affair." They had just celebrated twenty-two years of marriage when they came over to my home to offer their thoughts about the success of their marriage. Louise opened with one of the Bahá'í prayers for marriage, and I asked them to tell their story.

Bob had gone to the Yukon in 1980. He noted that during that time he knew that his first marriage was over, and had begun to pray, intensely, for a "new mate."

Shortly afterwards, his friend said, "Hey, have you heard about that Louise Profeit?"

He met Louise in Mayo. She had three little girls from a former common-law relationship. I asked if Bob and Louise had been attracted right away.

Bob said, "I didn't feel anything instant."

Louise told him, "You drove me to the airport."

Bob, surprised, answered, "Oh did I?"

Louise said, "I had been a Bahá'í for a year and a half. Prior to that, I had been alone for five years, with three small daughters. I was very particular. There were no romances. But then I had the bounty of going to Chicago to pray at the

Bahá'í Temple there, and I asked Bahá'u'lláh: Bring me my husband."

Meanwhile, Bob was still in Ontario, also saying prayers. Louise laughed and said, "Maybe the prayers collided!"

Louise had been taught the Bahá'í Faith by her friend Mark Wedge. This same friend asked Bob to go to Mayo to speak at a Bahá'í meeting. Louise noted that it was a time of testing for her: she was trying to be loving to "my Bahá'í brothers and sisters, even those who were not Aboriginal."

Then, she said, "This white guy shows up."

She liked him. "He had a pleasant aura that melted that sickening feeling inside of me."

She was referring to the feeling of estrangement between the races. Louise noted, "After the Bahá'í talk, I went to a potluck dinner."

Her three girls were with her. Bob was sitting in "this big old easy chair" and something in my brain said, "That's the man you're going to marry."

She was startled, completely taken by surprise. Yet she noted, "There was something in him I was familiar with: that was his pain—the pain of separation. Both of us had been in prior relationships that had broken apart."

She was about to move from Mayo to Whitehorse. Bob drove her to the airport, and she noted that this was a "supportive move," something that she was not used to. He could offer assistance "in a comfortable way." She said, "He didn't realize that I had inner turmoil, and he calmed me somehow."

In Whitehorse, they worked together on a Bahá'í committee. One day they were out driving somewhere and she saw two ravens flying along beside them. They swooped down and criss-crossed in the air. Louise mimed how the birds had moved, with her hands. She said, "I knew then that something was cooking."

She had already been confirmed: there was a period when "I wondered if it was simply infatuation or vain imaginings," but she was getting excited to be with Bob. Of Bob, she noted, "The other beautiful thing about him is he would drive us home, or he would pick up my girls and take them to children's classes." At this point in our interview, she turned to him and said, "That was so sweet of you, honey."

Bob asked her daughters, one day, if they thought Louise would go to the movies. One said, "No, she can't afford it." Bob admits he was "fishing" for Louise's "availability."

They went to see the movie *Little Big Man*. Louise laughed and said, "I'd never been on a 'date' with Bob before. I wanted to look beautiful."

I observed that this was new territory.

Louise noted, "I think that was when Bob realized how independent I was. It was hard for him."

Bob questioned this.

Louise: "You don't recall saying, 'you're too damned independent?'"

Bob: "I said that?"

We were all roaring with laughter.

Bob said, "Well, you are—like we'd go for a walk, and you'd be way ahead of me."

I joked, "She still is!"

Bob noted, reflecting, "I did learn about strong women from my previous marriage. I was prepared to accept that it's a new age and that the man is not the boss anymore. My first wife was a strong, independent woman, and I think that prepared me to be with a strong woman. I was therefore prepared for Louise by my previous relationship."

Bob continued, "In Whitehorse, after a few months of spending time with Louise, I realized that something was growing in me towards Louise that I'd never felt before, and one day I said, 'I think I'm in love.'"

He explained, "I wasn't sure what love meant. Through the tests of divorce I came to the conclusion that I would never say that word unless I meant it. What I felt for Louise, it was like a baby being born."

"We were friends before, but then it was more."

Louise agreed, "We were getting to know one another, we just became more intimate as friends, it became a 'love affair,' and the affair was love."

Bob agreed, noting that they had to wait for a year to get married, due to legalities, and they were chaste, and "that was a test."

He added, "We wanted to start our relationship as a married couple. But then there was a miracle."

The required waiting period for a divorce was lengthy. They made a case to the Supreme Court of the Yukon. The judge asked why they didn't just live together like everybody else. They explained that they couldn't, that they were following Bahá'í law regarding chastity, and that they were abstaining from sex before marriage.

Louise said that she heard a story, later, through the grapevine, that the judge had gone home and consulted with his wife, who said that the couple was trying to uphold the institution of marriage. So, after forty years of never having changed his mind on a decision, the judge's secretary called on the Monday and told them that he had done so—a miracle!

Marriage and Stepparenting

Louise continued their story. "Part of my admiration for Bob stemmed from his manner and personality. He was a sweet, nice-looking man. He had a great affinity for children. You would always see him picking up babies and carrying them around the gatherings. Another thing I noticed was that he was always in the kitchen helping out with dishes. This was all very attractive. I knew any man I was involved with would have to support me with parenting. My eldest child was twelve, and my youngest was six."

I asked about stepparenting.

Louise told me, "The girls were angered that I'd left their father, and they would say to Bob, 'You're not our real father.' Bob would calmly answer them, 'Yes, that's true, I can never be your natural father, but I still have a spiritual obligation.'"

Louise noted that although living through her daughters' adolescence was hell, Bob supported her through it and "brought sense to it."

All the girls got into trouble, but Louise reflected, "I remember him saying, when I was beating myself up about it, 'Honey, you've done the best you know how.'"

Bob interjected, "You had no money; you supported them all by yourself."

Louise laughed, "No money, no honey, no security . . . but a lot of faith and prayers."

I asked about the girls now and discovered that their grandson Alexander, whom Bob and Louise have been raising since he was four, is Louise's daughter Krystal's son, and that Bob and Krystal are now quite close. Bob also noted that although the youngest daughter had stayed with them the longest, only two were now somewhat stable, with one even being in university.

Bob said that his approach was "tough love." There were "lines of what was unacceptable in our household, and if they didn't wish to uphold that, they would have to leave."

Louise noted, "Early in our marriage, we had some troubled years because these were my children, and he was bringing new standards. I had been a Bahá'í for less time than Bob, and a couple of times I packed and left for a night. We even had a joke about his style—'Robert's Rules of Order.' They were white man's rules. But some were God's rules, really. They were based on the Bahá'í standard."

They both noted that there were periods where "the cultural norms were tested" and added, "Being Bahá'ís made the difference." They were agreed on rules about chastity, children, and having no drugs or alcohol.

I asked them, in these times of trouble, "How did you work it out?"

Bob said, instantly, "Prayers, consultation—truly, when you put forth an argument, there may be a clash of opinions. . . ."

Love as Forgiveness

Louise picked up, "I learned—it was sometimes a struggle—how to say I'm sorry. I really understand forgiveness, 'you just forget!' You can't remember what the big war was about."

They agreed that prayers and commitment were essential. I asked how much time it would take, when they were upset, to calm down again.

Bob said, "Some times would take longer than others. You get into your own corner, you don't want to lose the battle because, if you give in, you're seen as weak."

He noted that they would sometimes spend days not talking. It was "very painful."

Louise added, "It took patience to work our way out of our pickles. Sometimes I did not want to talk. I needed to stew. Sometimes I wanted to consult the Assembly*. I wanted help."

Bob wondered aloud, "How did we get through those times? We used to fight—I thought as Bahá'ís we'd never have to fight, but we ended up fighting a lot!"

Louise responded, "That was an unrealistic and much too high expectation!"

I asked, "How did you deal with anger?"

Louise: "I get loud and passionate. My husband doesn't appreciate my passion, especially when I swear!" She mimicked Bob, "That's not very Bahá'í-like!"

I asked how that made her feel.

Louise: "It would make things worse, I'd tell him, 'You're not my judge, God is.'"

---

* The Local Spiritual Assembly, an elected body of nine Bahá'ís who administer the local Bahá'í community.

Bob would then say something like, "Well, it says very clearly in the writings. . . ."

We were laughing by this point, but I was curious about how they got over this.

Louise noted that the last ten years had been different. Bob speculated that it might be the responsibility of having Alexander. Both said, "Patience is another key, and so is the concept of give and take."

Bob noted quietly, "There aren't any things you do that bother me."

Louise grinned, "That's great!"

She added, "I think acceptance and patience have helped us. True love, that's what it is. True love is not being blindsided by our partner." She laughed and addressed her husband. "My God, I've got to be with you for eternity, I might as well get used to you now!"

Louise has a great sense of humor, and she is very witty, yet she was tender when she said, "Every year I make a conscious effort to reflect on what quality I love best about you."

Bob noted, "We went to a marriage counselor." Louise said that she had not found that very helpful, and Bob agreed.

We talked about marriages going through cycles, and Louise noted, "Now, we're in a nice cycle, but it is not without struggles."

It was clear that their struggles were shared, and solved, together. The affection between them was palpable. They represented one of the several marriages where one of the partners inherited children along with the marriage.

David and Ann Hall contributed some thoughts about love, which developed into sharing about the many years they had spent as Bahá'í "pioneers" in Papua New Guinea. They met at a chiropractic college, and as Ann notes, their marriage, now of almost thirty years' duration, has lasted in part because of common goals. They really like working together. Also, their four children have brought great joy to them, and while living in Papua New Guinea, they were also blessed to have "extras"—four more children from that country who lived with the Halls as part of the family. They wanted to offer these children an opportunity to get a better education than they might have otherwise had, and as Ann said, "In hindsight, it is probably one of the best things we ever did over there, the icing on the cake."

She also noted that although the quarter century they spent in Papua New Guinea had been spent in several areas of the country, she probably loved Alotau the most because they had their own children, as well as their extended family of children, living with them. They bought a bakery, and had "something that was ours," so Ann "felt like she was home."

Of David, Ann said, "I am his best friend." She noted that for her, and for women in general, she thought that there was a great ease of intimacy, where women share "as much or more with each other." But with David, she said, there is also lots of sharing and connection. David wrote and gave some details, since I had asked a follow-up question. I wondered how they had known, when they were going out together, that they could be sure of the marriage.

David answered, "Can anyone be sure? It's scary because you are making this huge step that society generally promotes as permanent, and there is no guarantee it will work out. It requires daily effort and lots of prayer. The Bahá'í books such as *A Fortress for Well-Being* and now others give us a great plan to follow and helpful ideas on how to build and maintain relationships. We read and studied these books. We served our faith, and we knew that our partner was committed to service of the faith. We were in love and blinded enough that we couldn't see the faults of the other."

David, among others, has noted the blinding effects of being "in love."

He added the following: "Years later, all of a sudden you have kids and jobs, and then stress and faults appear. We had three kids under five, and we realized we had to stick together because we were outnumbered. They were little, but they could cause lots of trouble! So again we overlooked our faults and just concentrated on the faults of our kids."

David and Ann are dear friends of mine. I met them when I lived in Papua New Guinea at age twenty-one. I can just hear David's laughter and see his grin, in my mind's eye, as he says this, since I have seldom seen a couple more in love with their children and more committed to the welfare of all children.

As David said, "Occasionally we would blame one ancestor or another for our kids' weird behavior, but in the end the kids turned out quite well, and we took credit. We even had another in our later years to accompany us into old age and keep us from finding fault with each other for a few more years."

This is a great description of putting Ayron Hall's surprise appearance on the scene, when David and Ann were in their mid-forties. Ayron, their last child, is now in middle school in the Halls' new home in the southern United States. David added more detail to his thoughts about their marriage: "After twenty-nine years, we have greatly matured because we each see our own faults with a clarity that, as youth, we never had."

I note that here, David was speaking for himself and was referring to seeing his own faults, not Ann's. This seems to be a key for many of the couples: personally taking responsibility for their respective growth and avoiding blame.

He added, somewhat wryly, "We know we are just damn lucky to have someone to love us at all."

I enjoyed hearing about the Halls' experiences overseas. Of their almost thirty years of marriage, twenty-five have been spent in Papua New Guinea (PNG), a subject Ann had touched on.

David: "Pioneering was something we knew we were going to do even before we were married. We pioneered to Inman, South Carolina, when we married. When we graduated from college we pioneered to PNG, and we kept pioneering within the country to more isolated areas until we ended up on a sixty-five acre island."

He continued, "We can't imagine what our lives would have been like if we had not pioneered. Probably we would be wealthy, with insurance, retirement plans, and Ann would have a fast sports car. That's why we can't imagine it."

At this stage of David's account, I was laughing out loud. Anyone who knows Ann would find the image of Ann in a sports car quite distracting. Ann is a tall and beautiful blonde. Imagining Ann driving a sports car must have given both of them some fun!

David continued:

During the first ten years we spent in PNG, we lived in towns with large numbers of expatriates and quite a few pioneers. The pioneers grew close—we all had families with children, and we socialized together. PNG's expatriate community, especially the men, usually drank a lot, and could never quite deal with non-drinkers like the Bahá'ís. When we moved to Alotau we were the only pioneers. It was an area of the country where local people would often associate with expatriates socially, and there was a historical context of doing so due to some maverick missionaries. We became much more involved in the lives of Papua New Guineans and much more a part of a specific tribe of Papua New Guinean people.

As Ann had mentioned, Alotau was where the Hall family had felt the most "at home." Their family consists of eldest son Solomon, daughter Amelia, son Jordan, and youngest son Ayron, in addition to Solomon's wife Gloria and Amelia's husband Shahram. David continued his explanation of their expanded family life:

This was when Roger Duari came and lived with us for a year to do his grade 6, and he and Solomon became best friends. Our youngest at that time was Jordan, and he was the first to call Roger his brother and support him in family wrestling matches. Our daughter began to hang out with women and look after babies—she was only five or six at the time. She became a real PNG girl—she could move easily from the village, where she washed dishes in the river and carried water in buckets on her head to the kitchen up the hill, to the town, or to the U.S.A. on holidays.

The Hall children also have extraordinary stories of their years in Papua New Guinea. I hope they will write them someday. David continued explaining their lives in PNG: "Ann developed deep friendships with a number of PNG women that has extended through the years. This was at a time when the kids were old enough to leave them with Dad and they would still survive. She spent days and nights working with women on the Provincial Council of Women and other activities and traveling to the villages for Bahá'í activities. This is what she was talking about when she says women share so much, and she developed such intimate connections with women at that time in Alotau."

David summarized his thoughts with the following: "It's good you talked to Ann on the phone instead of me last week. You might not have gotten very good material from me, but Ann has gotten us started—she is the one who keeps us all happy and together."

Ann reciprocated, in kind: "I've got to pick myself off the floor after reading David's epistle to you . . . as you probably have already figured . . . if we did have any problems it was his incredible sense of fun that got us out!"

As someone who has been friends with David and Ann Hall for over a quarter of a century, I can say that while I appreciate David's loving accolade to his wife, they are both inspiring to be around, and the ease and joy they bring to their marriage and family life is an inspiration for anyone.

Love as Selflessness

Stuart North is of British background and also offered a perspective on love. He talked about it in terms of its changing nature and offered interesting definitions about love and its expression. Stuart has been married to his French-Canadian wife, Adelie, for over thirty years. Stuart has told me, "Falling in love seems to be an intense physical and emotional attraction to another person of the opposite sex. When we are young it is very intense and often blinds us to the flaws in the other person's character. Love is more pure and selfless and comes with maturity. In a marriage, love involves caring for and being supportive of one's spouse and children. Love is a spiritual virtue, whereas falling in love is more a part of our animal nature. Ideally, love should be a major part of the falling in love process, which is the mutual attraction of two people to one another."

This mutual attraction is expressed eloquently by Suzanne Schuurman when she speaks of the early days of her marriage to her husband Hubert and of the sense of discovery of each other:

Writing about the early days of our marriage, after over forty years, I tend to make assumptions and gloss over areas that were intensely vital. Early married life was full of wonder and surprises; for weeks I was intrigued to see Hubert shave in the morning and delighted when he played the flute for me. Hubert was a great hiking companion; together we enjoyed poetry and classical music. Irritations that were to remain all through our married life surfaced that first year as well. Yet it is the wonder of living with someone you love that I most remember. A memory surfaces of us going to see a film together—it must have been shortly after our wedding. When the house lights went on, and I looked at my handsome husband sitting beside me, I was filled with such awe at God's bounty that I remember the incident to this day.

Daily Love in Marriage

Each of the couples who told their stories emphasized the "dailiness" of love. Each mentioned, in some way or other, the idea that those aspects of the person that most delighted them were the ones they thought about when they needed to remind themselves of the reasons they had wanted to be married to this person. In the little things, in the accumulation of moments such as those described by Suzanne, were the recipe for joy. Love was—and is—a daily event in practice.

Pam and Jeff Stellick commented on this aspect of daily love in their marriage. In their case, there was a slight difference in the way they related their story. When I asked them, after thirty years of marriage, what the secret was to their marital success, Pam joked, "We're lazy." We laughed, but she explained that she really thought that in many of the tests they had faced, they never wanted to make a big issue out of a little one. As a result, they always chose to ignore the small stuff that came up during their years together.

The Stellicks and I were at a Bahá'í gathering together, and they were chosen as guinea pigs for a game. With their chairs back to back, they were asked to remove their shoes. The man conducting the game then gave one of Pam's shoes to Jeff, and vice versa. He then went through a series of questions. When the individual thought that the answer was "me," he or she would lift the appropriate shoe in the air. When the answer to the question was the spouse, the shoe belonging to that person was lifted. If they thought the question should be answered, "Both," they lifted both shoes. The questions included, "Who does most of the cooking?", "Who cleans the bathroom the best after a bath?", "Who is the grumpiest in the morning?", and so on.

We had a lot of fun watching Jeff and Pam answer these questions without looking at each other to see what the other was saying. They almost always agreed. Both, for example, were sure that it was Jeff who is more grouchy in the morning. They agreed that they shared cooking and cleaning fairly equally. Pam and I chatted after the game, and she asked if they had answered similarly. I assured her that they had.

Pam wrote to me later that she and Jeff had discussed the game and agreed on what they thought of it. She said, "It was interesting for us to go through that game. We were pleasantly surprised to find that we were mostly in sync on the little issues brought out in the game. It's easy to not think about such things during our day-to-day business, but the exercise boosted our awareness of the connection we have in both the little and big things. It shows how connected we are in the daily love of our marriage."

The Barrows confirmed the necessity of a daily loving connection; when asked, "What habits or practices have contributed to the success of your marriage?" they answered, "Having a private conversation of at least thirty minutes every day—no matter what—is one of our secrets. We always get up and have a conversation all to ourselves early in the morning over coffee or tea—either in bed or outdoors on the veranda if the weather is good."

Barry and Marilyn Smith, Americans who have lived almost all of their married life in Central America, noted, "We think that we established good foundational blocks in our early marriage, and one of those foundations is praying for each other daily." This is an element of love, for many couples.

The Smiths also noted,

'Abdu'l-Bahá has said, with regard to love between two individuals, that "each sees in the other the Beauty of God reflected in the soul, and finding this point of similarity, they are attracted to one another in love."[1] Both of us think the attraction He describes is "falling in love," especially when it is at many levels: physical, emotional, intellectual, psychological. We frequently say to each other, "I love you," which fosters security and well-being. Our love is different and even better today—more comfortable, in a sense—than thirty years ago when we married. It is based on mutual experiences, sacrifice, and suffering. We use the word *love* in our relationship more now than we did when first married because this shared life has deepened our attachment to each other. Therefore, the love we feel for each other is greater.

Coral and Ovidio Gomez noted that one aspect of love is being aware of each other's needs. As Coral explained, "Sometimes Ovidio will do something for me that is normally not in our daily routine, or I will do something for him that is not common. It just gets a little interesting. I think it's important not to get boring."

Reginald Barrow, whose marriage also crosses culture, noted, "Love is raising someone else's well-being to be more important than your own," and "Falling in love is the realization that the other person is really a part of you more than a separate entity."

June Barrow added, "I would agree with Reg but add that it's one of those things that can't really be explained but makes everything work, like electricity or light."

Love as Respect

Peter and Muguette Brady have emphasized that mutual respect is the foundation of their love for one another, and that this respect is in part based on their ability to communicate by not only speaking but genuinely hearing the other person and paying close attention to each other. This ability to communicate is one that Peter commented came to him as an important value in growing up with a mother who was a single parent. Peter offered these thoughts on love:

The definitions are important, but only in the way we jointly define them. Part of love is respect for each other. Recently my wife said one of the things that attracted her to me was that I respected her as a person. Because I was raised by a mother who was a single parent, I had occasions to see women in situations usually not seen or noticed by men. I have always had a genuine respect for women and the difficulties they face. Nobility of character is not exclusively a masculine quality. My mother and many of her friends demonstrated this to me very clearly—but because the status of women is unfairly and blatantly lower than that of men, this quality in women is often ignored or overlooked.

I found it interesting that Peter conflated love with respect. This concept overlapped with an explanation offered by another respondent. Greg and Ginny Kintz noted the different backgrounds from which they had come. This is Ginny, writing on behalf of them both after they used the questions I had asked as the basis for a conversation during a long drive:

> We came from very different childhood experiences. I came from a large family whose parents were committed to their marriage (they just celebrated their fifty-fifth anniversary). Greg is an only child who was raised by a single mother and a father who was married five times, his mother being number four. I wanted a marriage like my parents had; he looked to examples of strong marriages and the teachings of the Bahá'í Faith because he wanted what his mother didn't have. Because of her bad experiences with men, however, she consciously raised him to respect women and to be a good husband. I think I have the best husband there could possibly ever be!

Love as Friendship

Suzanne Schuurman was one of several people who noted that each individual in a couple always brings different life experiences and different perceptions into a relationship. When a couple is more interested in finding a united point of view than in entering into any kind of adversarial scorekeeping, they are able to overcome differences of opinion and find common ground more easily. On the other hand, "winning" a battle in order to lose the war is counterproductive to the long-term health of the marriage. Hence, it is better to focus on finding unity rather than dwelling on disunity:

Why does our marriage work? Love is a great binding force, but in times of stress it needs divine assistance. Both Hubert and I come from a European background, he Dutch, and I Polish. This provides a common framework. Both of us were affected in our childhood by the Second World War, he during the Nazi occupation of Holland and I through wandering with my mother in Europe ahead of the invasion forces until coming to Canada. These shared early impressions helped us to understand the after-echoes of wartime traumas in our adult lives. Our common love for classical music, especially opera, as well as our love for painting and literature is a garden of delight from which we both find inspiration and pleasure. Most constant, pervasive and all-enveloping is the love we share. It is the adhesive force that binds us, cheers us, and brightens our days together. I feel confident that it will light our way in the other worlds of God as well. We have a close companionship and intimate friendship; perhaps in the years remaining to us we will develop "even as a single soul."[2]

A few of the couples who shared their stories with me had met at a very young age, including Greg and Ginny. This was of some interest to me, since there is a popular wisdom that suggests that young marriages are predisposed to failure. The Kintzes, the Gordon Epps, the Bowies, the Dorans, and the Slobodians—all married young. Ginny told me, "We met when we were eighteen and married when we were both twenty, and so we have 'grown up' with each other. We can honestly say that we are best friends as much as we are lovers and marriage partners. Now that our children are on their own for the most part, we are starting all over again as a couple and are discovering that it is great fun."

The spiritual framework of love is embedded within many of the definitions of these long-term married couples, but it is not without romance. I enjoyed Bruce Filson's view: "Love is only real as a reflection of God's love. The other romantic love is a dangerous mirage. But it's amazing what kind of mileage you can get out of chocolates and flowers and silly stuff."

His wife, Margaret Bremner, quoted Antoine de St-Exupéry, who said, 'Love does not consist in gazing at each other but in looking outward together in the same direction.'"[3]

She also notes, "'Love' means wishing for the other person as good or better than you would wish for yourself. It also means encouraging and supporting his or her spiritual progress—this is *very* important. The idea of romantic love—which ultimately entails nonfulfillment, but people prefer not to think of that part!—is dopey and probably dangerous."

Janis Zrudlo added her version of the balance between the practical and the romantic:

Leo and I met when he was a student of architecture at the University of Manitoba. Before his last year at university, he had come to Ottawa to work for the summer with the Federal Government, designing an airport for the North-west Territories. We were introduced to each other by mutual architect friends. We have been married forty-four years, and I have to say it was a very rational decision on my part. I remember thinking that here was someone that I could face over the breakfast table each morning and not feel the slightest sense of letdown. Besides, he drove a nifty sports car and sang Peggy Lee songs as we went along.

Janis indicated that she was smiling as she was writing. She has a warm and wonderful smile, which I am sure Leo enjoys seeing over the breakfast table, as well.

All of the couples expressed the idea that love changed over time and that being seduced by the plethora of ideas about romantic love available in pop culture could be very blinding to the qualities that were more likely to sustain long-term marriages. Marriage was not just a social contract between individuals—it was the connecting of family systems. Love was defined in broad terms and was considerably implicated in family life.

Love Between the Races

I would like to share Margaret Varner's story of her meeting with William:

When I met William Varner, I had been coordinating a Bahá'í project for a few months in a very poor area on the eastern shore of Maryland. Many other people had come and gone. He was different. I was overwhelmed by his desire to serve the people we were teaching and by his sincere love for them. After the second day of serving together, I knew he was my husband, and I guess he felt something too. We were married two months later.

That was thirty-three years, five children, and ten grandchildren ago. It hasn't always been easy, but nothing worth having is easy. We've had to work hard and trust in God's will. We're very, very different in many ways, but that's probably why we've learned so much from each other.

Here, Margaret cited a comment from the late wife of Shoghi Effendi, who was the grandson of 'Abdu'l-Bahá and someone whom Bahá'ís hold in enormous respect: "Rúḥíyyih Khánum says that marriage is like the rough pebbles in a stream. Years of being rubbed against each other polishes them into smooth gems. We've got lots of smoothing yet to do, but I like the analogy."

Margaret continued their story: "I am a white American by birth. My mother was of Jewish heritage; most of her mother's side of the family died in concentration camps in Czechoslovakia and Austria during World War II. Her father's family was from England, but their ancestors were originally from France. My father's father was German and his mother was Irish. I am very grateful for the fact that my parents taught me that there is only one race—the human race—and that we are all God's children."

Margaret, like many of the others who have shared their stories, embraced the Bahá'í Faith and its teachings as a young woman:

Since becoming a Bahá'í as a teenager, I see myself as a world citizen. Being married to an African-American for thirty-three years and raising five children has taught me a lot about the racism that is systemic in our country. I literally had no problems in American society until I became aware of the color line. As a child, our family hosted a Nigerian exchange student for four or five years during the early 1960s. When we took Olatunji to the country club to which we belonged, we children had no idea that this was anything out of the ordinary. When we jumped in the pool, everyone else got out. Our parents called us to all get out, and we left the country club with our parents laughing loudly. We were laughing, too, because they were laughing, but we didn't know what the joke was until we got home and our parents explained it to us. We never went back to the country club.

During our marriage we've had a number of situations that were challenging, including people shooting at our dog and telling us we would be next, not wanting to rent to us, not serving us, etc., but those situations only made us closer and more determined. Because of my color, I am able to move freely about and enjoy the services and benefits that are sometimes denied to people of color in this society. When I am with members of my family I am treated differently than I am when I am alone. I've been called all kinds of things when I've taken a walk with our children.

When our bouncy, cheerful, five-year-old was called "nigger" at a Little League baseball game, and our oldest daughter was accused of theft and frisked just because she used the bathroom in a store in a white neighborhood, and our nephews were beaten by policemen on their way home from Thanksgiving dinner, and my husband was thrown to the ground by four drunk teenagers, kicked in the head and in the back and told to go back to Africa (that was in the early '90s in Canada) it begins to sink in that we really do live in a racist society.

So many of the couples in this book have spoken to the development of their relationship as a process of loving one another through the tests which life brings. No one was more eloquent, I thought, than Margaret, in describing what she and William have faced as a mixed-race couple. Margaret continued, "This racism is not as evident today as it was years ago, when we were first married, or when our children were young. Things are changing, but I'm still aware of the difference, because I've lived it for years." About their family, Margaret noted,

The issue of raising interracial children is a whole other topic. Many interracial children have excruciating identity problems as they try to navigate their way in a world that is overwhelmingly black or white. Our children were very fortunate in several ways: there are lots of them! Not only did we have five children in seven years, but our children had cousins—literally by the dozen—who were also interracial, the same ages, and living next door or around the corner while all of them were growing up. In other words, they had a huge support group without even realizing that they needed one.

Such support also came from their faith community: "They were also all Bahá'ís and therefore were taught about the oneness of mankind from an early age. They still faced some identity struggles but nothing in comparison to what most interracial children face. They were asked by classmates if they were really panda bears or zebras, told that black and white couldn't live together, that it was 'against the Bible,' asked if they 'were supposed to be white,' and if it was true that their parents slept together. These are just a few of the things they had to endure while growing up."

In reading Margaret's narrative, the following section made me think of the injunction of the Bahá'í writings—"When a thought of war comes, oppose it by a stronger thought of peace."[4]

Margaret told how their children dealt with their experiences:

Usually they just thought it was funny and enlightened their classmates about the oneness of mankind. The little girl who bragged to one of our daughters about how her father was a Klansman didn't get much of a response, however.

Having said all that, I must say that all of these experiences have greatly influenced my own spiritual growth in a positive way. I've learned so much from my husband and children that I never would have known if I hadn't been interracially married. I'm also thankful to the countries of the United States and Canada for the freedoms we have here. There are actually very few countries in the world where citizenship is not based on ethnicity or race. The

United States was also founded on freedom of religion, which is very important to me. I'm very thankful that I can be a Bahá'í and that I can be married to the person of my choice. This is not an option everywhere in the world.

Margaret, who is known as Peggy to her friends—of whom I am proud to be one—concluded, "Someday mankind will see not only the America but also the world that Martin Luther King, Jr. and Malcolm X both described and for which they both gave their lives. They both saw a society where character and spiritual qualities of the soul were more important than a person's pigmentation. The Bahá'í Faith tells us that that day will come. It will be the fulfillment of the promise of the Lord's Prayer: 'Thy kingdom come, Thy will be done on earth as it is in heaven.'"

3

FAMILY AND CONSENT

*Marriage is dependent upon the consent of
both parties. Desiring to establish love, unity
and harmony amidst Our servants, We have conditioned
it, once the couple's wish is known, upon the
permission of their parents, lest enmity and rancor
should arise amongst them. And in this We have yet other
purposes. Thus hath Our commandment been ordained.*

Bahá'u'lláh

Many couples I interviewed spoke of the role of family—specifically, parents—in their marriages. Some praised the support their parents gave them while at the same time noting the need to have one's own personal space, apart from the extended family. Still others told of the process of getting their parents' approval for marriage. From the interviews with the various couples, it appeared that support from parents was a crucial step in determining the happiness of many married couples.

Wisdom of Requiring the Consent of Parents

Having a family's blessing for a marriage is an old idea that is found in many cultures. In the Bahá'í teachings, the founder of the Bahá'í Faith made it a binding law that in order for a couple to marry, the parents of both the bride and groom-to-be must first give their consent for the marriage to take place. The consent of all four parents is required before the wedding. The Bahá'í writings clearly state, "First thou must choose one who is pleasing to thee."[1] Then, the consent of each of the couple's living parents is required. This law of consent may at first seem to be an anachronistic and arbitrary dictum, but for several of the couples mentioned in this book, it provided the glue that held their marriages together in the face of adversity.

The reasons for seeking consent from one's parents are made clear in the Bahá'í writings. Shoghi Effendi, the Guardian of the Bahá'í Faith, has written,

> Bahá'u'lláh has clearly stated the consent of all living parents is required for a Bahá'í marriage. . . . This great law He has laid down to strengthen the social fabric, to knit closer the ties of the home, to place a certain gratitude and respect in the hearts of children for those who have given them life and sent their souls out on the eternal journey towards their Creator. . . . In present-day society the exact opposite is taking place: young people care less and less for their parents' wishes, divorce is considered a natural right, and obtained on the flimsiest and most unwarrantable and shabby pretexts. People separated from each other, especially if one of them has had full custody of the children, are only too willing to belittle the importance of the partner in marriage also responsible as a parent for bringing those children into this world.[2]

Thus, the wisdom of the Bahá'í teaching on gaining consent from parents is that it strengthens the bonds of the family and promotes unity between the couple and their parents.

The issue of gaining consent from one's parents before marriage is much different from the typical American idea of what a marriage should be. Edna Nablo commented on the idea of parental consent as part of the decision to marry: "In our individualistic North American culture, which often exalts the rights of the individual above the rights and needs of society in general, this is a difficult provision to understand. No parent wants to alienate his or her child, and unless the child has been raised with the expectation that his or her parents will have some input after the choice of a marriage partner is made, a refusal may be just too great a test, and it may alienate the child. I think some parents are unwilling to take the risk, and they consent when they really feel it would be better to say no. So, courage is needed."

Edna went on: "We are all products of our culture, and the fact that my husband and I have accepted Bahá'u'lláh's teachings does not mean that the cultural influences of our upbringing cease to be operative. So, while our minds may fully accept the wisdom of the Bahá'í way, our hearts may be telling us something different." Edna's narrative is based, in part, on experience with one of her children. Coral de Gomez is the fifth of the six Nablo children, and she met and married her husband Ovidio while doing Bahá'í service in Haifa. Coral and Ovidio understand, very powerfully, the importance of family unity.

Ovidio Gomez came from a devout Christian family in Honduras. When he encountered the Bahá'í faith, he decided to do service at its World Center in Haifa in order to better understand the new faith he had embraced. During his time there, he met Coral. She had left Canada because for three years, she had wanted to marry a particular young man. Her parents did not feel comfortable with the potential for this marriage, and as Bahá'í parents are given the right of consent by the writings of their faith, they asked Coral to wait for a year more, separately, from the young man. If, at the end of that time, she still felt so strongly about marrying him, they might reconsider their decision.

Coral decided that serving in Haifa would be a good way to pass the year. Several months later, her parents received a letter from her. It was a passionate expression of thanks for their wisdom. She had realized, separately from her boyfriend, that their marriage would not have worked. And, although she had not been searching for someone, there was another young man she had met in whom she was interested. He was from Honduras, not far from where her parents lived in Belize.

Many phone calls and letters were exchanged, and Coral's parents had a "gut feeling" that this one was a good match. They gave consent, and Ovidio and Coral were married.

The Gomez family now includes five children. I interviewed the couple for the purposes of this book, and what struck me about the interview was Ovidio's words of love for his wife's ability to adapt to his culture and to love his birth family. Ovidio comes from a close-knit family in which he is the youngest of eight children. His father passed away while Ovidio was in Haifa, and this remains a source of grief to him, but he maintained close ties with his mother, Julia, until her passing in May 2006. He also remains close with his siblings. Coral also came from a family with numerous children, and both families became friends, despite—or perhaps because of—language difficulties (Coral's parents speak only English; Ovidio's mother spoke only Spanish.) They all made efforts to understand one another, and this has provided some of the foundation for the sustained love for this couple. As Coral expressed it, "We don't have problems in the in-law area, and I think beyond love, we actually like each other, and my mother-in-law loved me."

Ovidio added his comments:

> Just because you don't understand a different culture doesn't mean you can't adjust. Eventually, you do adjust, and Coral did really well. My family's Christian, and Coral always joined in our celebration in Honduras without compromising her principles. . . . She learned to respect and then to like the customs, and she ate the food. I think it helped living in Santa Lucia—we had opportunities to serve and to help others, and the community is always praising her on a daily basis. I miss not living in a community where you are helping others. Here, we live in relative isolation. You get tired when you are always doing community service, but it's worth it, and people remind me, "what a wife you have," "you are so lucky," just in case I forget [He laughed]. Family and friends also remind me. They love her, and she helps all the time.

Coral told a story of the cultural adjustments they encountered when they were getting to know one another:

> When Ovidio and I got married he had the stereotype of a North American woman that couldn't cook or clean and was not home-oriented. Before we got married, I went over to visit him, and he cooked for me because he thought I couldn't cook. I didn't know he thought that, and it's to

his credit that he still wanted to marry me. I think in some ways he was making a sacrifice because he was used to being tended. Then after we were married he said, "Aren't you going to make the bed?" and I said, "No," and he said "Okay." I told him if he wanted the bed made since he was the last one out of it, he could make it. Then one day I cooked chicken, and he found out I could cook, and he has barely cooked since! But I don't mind because I like cooking, and he helps a lot with other things. But when he cooks, it's man food, you know, meat.

Coral laughed and added, "And I can read his mind. I don't know if that's a good thing, but I always know what he's thinking, and more or less vice-versa."

Requesting Consent to Marry

Consent of parents to a marriage is an important part of the Bahá'í teachings; its intent is, among other aspects, to strengthen family unity. But what happens if a couple's parents do not want to give their consent right away? Sometimes the process of asking for consent, in itself, leads to new opportunities for connection between a couple and others and places them in the context of a broader support system. Helen de Marsh's story of attaining consent to marry Maury Miloff illustrates this idea:

We suffered through what seemed like an interminable period of waiting for consent, during which time we came to know ourselves and families a lot better, became more confirmed in our faith and matured in general. I remember us approaching John Robarts, a distinguished Bahá'í, with our terrible dilemma and pouring our hearts out to him, from the point of view of our suffering, and his loving response. He said to us, "Your parents seem to love you a very great deal." I believe he said it a number of times, and it had the wonderful effect of helping us gain perspective on their concerns. He and his wife Audrey personified the one soul in two bodies concept so completely, and we could really hear what they had to say.

Of course, the fact that Helen and Maury were willing to try to see the concerns of their parents also speaks to the integrity of their own behavior as young people. Marriage, in such circumstances, does not become an act of rebellion or of insistence but is inclusive of and understanding of parental concerns.

Gillian Mottahed shared some of the challenges of getting consent to marry, since her parents were estranged: "When I explained the need for consent to Mom, she gave her consent. Then she contacted my father, and he came to see me while I was at work. My father had been estranged from the family for years, and he was amazed at the fact that he needed to give consent to the marriage of a daughter that he hardly knew."

For Parviz's family, consent was also an issue. Parviz went home for the summer after seven years in England. He knew he wanted to marry Gillian, but his father was against it. Parviz recalled, "He was not against the person so much as the idea. The idea of intercultural marriage was rather new in those days. It was something that was not usually done."

Upon completion of his bachelor's degree, Parviz was welcomed back to Iran by everyone. He said, "I was partied out!"

At one point, his parents started to introduce him to female friends of the family to look for a suitor. The hiatus of seven years away from Iran had molded his character to a Western model of thinking about courtship. Parviz said, "I was introduced to a lot of people. Everyone seemed like a sister to me, so I said to my parents, 'I'll talk one-to-one, no chaperone.'"

His father, who was used to a more traditional style of courtship—where the man and woman are not left by themselves—said, "Can't be done."

So Parviz told his father, "If I like a girl more than the one I already met, then I'll consider her. Otherwise I will go without a partner as long as it takes." He noted, "But I was totally desperate for consent to marry Gillian, and I had a trick up my sleeve."

Parviz continued,

> My mother had a cousin who was educated in Beirut and was very familiar with Western culture. She was highly respected, both within and outside the family. I thought that she was the key to unlocking this impasse, and I asked her to talk to my dad. So she did, and after a long period of discussion, my father gave his consent to my marriage with Gillian. My mother dashed upstairs and picked up her own engagement ring for me to give to Gillian as the sign of approval and proceeded to make the arrangement

for our wedding at an appropriate time. This was a symbolic gesture. We were dealing with a different culture: in a Persian family, the marriage of the first son is very important. It was hard for my parents to communicate with Gillian, though my mother had some knowledge of the English language. My father had a lot of difficulties with communicating with Gillian.

It's ironic, my father later had a tremendous relationship with Gill. When we were in Saskatoon, one day my father and Gill were shelling peas together. My mother suddenly appeared on the scene and commented that she never had seen my father do any "kitchen task." Of course Gill had learned the language, and she asked him, what are you doing, and he said, "I'm shelling peas."

Parviz laughed after recounting this part of the story. Gill said, "I learned enough Farsi, pidgin Farsi. Mrs. Faizi was my first teacher. I was fortunate; she taught me reading, writing and speaking. It was a great start, and of course I learned enough Farsi during my nearly three years' stay in Iran."

She added, "Parviz was in many ways anglicized, but he always managed to keep the balance, whereas for myself I was fortunate because the family I married into were welcoming, and soon I was at home with all of them."

Culture, parents, family, children: all play a part in the unfolding of successful marriages. Bob and Louise Profeit-LeBlanc also spoke to the significance of cultural differences. She is a First Nations Canadian from the Yukon Territory; he is white. I asked them to explain further the impact this had had on their marriage.

Bob felt that their different backgrounds were a blessing. He noted, "I wanted to marry a nonwhite person; it's always a blessing. 'Abdu'l-Baha encouraged interracial marriages. Louise, on the other hand, didn't get so 'attached' to culture. It didn't matter all that much to her."

Louise said that her priorities had shifted. "Before I was a Bahá'í, I practiced my Aboriginality but later I didn't have time for doing the ceremonial sweats and so on. I had to sacrifice some of that for the larger task at hand, the Bahá'í Faith."

Bob added, "You weren't all about 'being Indian.'"

Louise said, "I would rather practice. The Indian way is part of me, inside me, ingrained in me, I don't have to tell people about it."

Bob: "I love the culture."

Louise told him, "You say you love the sense of humor."

Bob answered, "You can have a lot of fun with Native people, be yourself, be relaxed."

Louise continued, "I came from the village culture, for example, when I am at your house, just hanging out, I just take my leave, just slip out. This business of goodbye, and thank you, it's not in my frame of reference. If someone comes over with a big chunk of meat, you just say, 'oh, I'll put it over here' and later you cook it and share it. What is courtesy? Just words? Sometimes this was a bone of contention between us."

She explained, "Bob wanted me to send thank you cards, like to his mom, but being raised in a community where you do something, not words—my grandma would say, what's that word, 'Thank you?'"

I laughed and thanked them for the interview, but we joked that I'd already cooked dinner, and Louise laughed, "I had to sing for my supper!"

Louise combines her cultural tradition and her faith, serving both: professionally, she directs acquisitions of Aboriginal art for an important group in Canada's capital city. She is an internationally renowned Native storyteller and also served for several years on the National Spiritual Assembly of the Bahá'ís of Canada.

Several of these marriages are working towards accomplishing the central Bahá'í principle of unity in diversity. Marital relationships increase connection with many families of differing backgrounds. Coral de Gomez's willingness to listen to the wishes of her parents contributed to the joy she now feels with Ovidio. Each of them is loved by the other's family. Maury and Helen's wish to commence their own marriage, within the context of obedience to Bahá'í teachings on consent, strengthened the family bonds throughout their marriage. Gillian and Parviz's Mottahed's obedience ended up uniting two very different families into one. The law of consent contributes to unity, which then offers a wonderful support system to couples.

Equality in the Family

I have wondered about the issue, in marriage, of "who yields?" In times past, before social attempts at demonstrating the equality of men and women in marriage, this would not have been a question. It would, invariably, have been the woman who yielded. In many of these stories, women have yielded to their husband's desires. The Universal House of Justice has written, "There are, therefore, times when a wife should defer to her husband, and times when a husband should defer to his wife, but neither should ever unjustly dominate the other."[3]

Susan Eghrari Moraes shared thoughts about gender equality in marriage:

> I think there can be a tendency towards domination. Usually we think of marriage as a polarized relationship where a winner must be recognized. For many years, mostly when our three children were small, I tried to be the pacifier of the relationship. I thought that if my opinions about, let's say, the choice of the children's school, the use of money in certain utilities, a weekend trip, was clashing with my husband's opinion, it was better not to continue expressing them. However, suppressing my individuality would not bring a balance to our relationship. We learned to discuss the matters, talk about them, have patience to listen, and draw out conclusions for our future. We learned to see only the good qualities of each other and to tell these good qualities to our children. Going back to the example of the two circles, if one just yields, there is no intersection, only one tangential point, which implies more conflicts.

Susan was speaking about one of the central tenets of the Bahá'í Faith—the principle of the equality of women and men. The equality of the sexes seemed to be greatly in the consciousness of those who had been married for many years. Equality was connected with respect. And, as Maury Miloff said, of their marriage, "Perhaps a strong sense of gender equality on my part helped as well. I don't think Helen ever felt particularly oppressed or restricted."

Marilyn Smith commented on experiences for her and Barry that were helpful in understanding the processes involved in making decisions based not on the desire of one individual but on the needs of the family as a whole. She said,

> One time a friend asked me if I ever regretted sacrificing my journalism education career while Barry could pursue his. I was taken aback by the question, as it had never crossed my mind because the decision was made according to what we thought would be best for the well-being of the family. I had decided before having children to sacrifice a few years to be at home with them, as we both thought that it would contribute to having emotionally and spiritually happy children. When seeking ways to have a proactive role in their education, I heard about Montessori preschool education and pursued training in that. With moving to a home-front pioneering post, elementary education through home-schooling for five children was required, and I learned how to do that effectively. After their departure from home, I learned how to administrate a development project. That original "sacrifice" opened up many opportunities and learning experiences that prepared and allowed me to later on serve the Bahá'í Faith full-time. Our Creator works in mysterious ways.

The salient factor appears to be choice. There is always, of course, the issue of power, but none of the couples who shared their views on this subject—and there were several—appeared to have issues with one person dominating the other. I was interested in the perceptions of some of the women, including Marilyn Smith, that in choosing to make the changes they did to their lives, and sometimes to their professions, they did not give in to unreasonable demands made by a more powerful husband. Nor did the husbands feel that they had been pressured by their wives. Rather, in a consultative manner, couples made decisions together for their families. Marilyn's viewpoint, that such "sacrifices" were not really sacrificial because they led to other, positive, and unexpected outcomes, is an interesting one to consider in the context of current social issues. The equality of women and men in the marriage implied a fully consultative model where both wife and husband felt that their views were being heard, respected, and applied for the best interests of the marriage. There were no competitions between partners, but a genuine effort to find cooperation over difficult life decisions.

This was, in my thinking, an aspect of the practical application of the core value in Bahá'í teaching of the principle of unity in diversity, with broad implications for the needs of the whole family having greater importance, on occasion, than individualistic tendencies that might have been learned from the dominant culture. Sometimes it seems that North American culture, with which I am most familiar, can appear to stress individual needs over those of the family or the community.

I learned a great deal from Marilyn's narrative about the importance of being able to see things from the perspective of the larger whole. "What do I want?" may not always be the best question for the sustenance of a successful marriage. More useful might be, "What do we both want that best serves both our individual hopes and our family needs?"

The Working Parents

Marilyn spoke about the importance of family and its example to the longevity of marriage: "One set of parents was married for fifty-eight years before Dad died. The other set has been married for fifty-seven years. Our parents' marriages have influenced greatly our expectations and perceptions. We grew up in a time when few mothers had to work or choose to work outside the home, and our neighbors were like an extended family. We assumed that we would be married for a long time, and so it has been."

The times in which we live have significantly changed from the time Marilyn describes here. Divorce has become more commonplace, and the fact that both partners work outside the home has made family life more complicated. Bahá'í teachings, along with many other philosophies in popular culture, encourage each partner in a marriage to have education and the ability to work at something that both interests them and is financially rewarding. Women are not excepted from this encouragement. In fact, the principle of women's equality with men in every aspect of life is frequently reiterated in Bahá'í writings. How do couples successfully juggle household sharing, making money, and choices?

In speaking about this topic, Marilyn noted, "One year, Barry basically lived alone for several months, and he discovered all the time it takes to prepare food, clean, shop, and launder clothes. Today, he willingly collaborates with me on all these responsibilities because he now has a greater appreciation and skill for doing them."

Every couple interviewed for this book remarked on a similar theme. When household tasks were shared, the chances were better for the creation of unity. Marilyn Smith talks of the process by which couples come to such ability to share: "The first turning point that we recall in our marriage occurred when we were pioneering in Puerto Rico with one infant daughter and a two-year-old daughter. With one child we had been able to travel teach actively together. With two children those occasions were limited. I was feeling unproductive."

Marilyn continued, "Barry knew I was unhappy, and neither one of us knew what to do. . . . Our prayers were answered, and the resolution came unexpectedly. One evening we had an opportunity to serve dinner for a Central American friend. When encouraged to ask any question, Barry articulated my concern. A dear family friend, Hedi Ahmadiyeh, cradling our infant in his arms, was able to enlighten and calm our hearts and souls." Marilyn recounted Hedi's advice:

He said that when we marry we become as one soul. He compared marriage and family to a bird and the husband and wife as the two wings. He explained that if one sacrifices so that the other can directly serve our goals, the spiritual bounties from sacrifice and service descend upon the whole family. He added that circumstances change during our married lives and that for some time one may be able to serve more directly, and then later the other will be freer to serve. Those few words had a permanent and life-long impact on our marriage, relationship, and family, thus widening the door for dedicating our lives to service.

This couple needed time, consideration, prayer, and advice in order to work out an arrangement that was acceptable to both. Marilyn elaborated at some length on the processes she and Barry had encountered. She said that they needed to find balance in their lives. They were doing a lot of work for the Bahá'í Faith, but some of this activity seemed to cut into Marilyn's ability to focus on the growing needs of their family. As she explained,

> It got to the point that when I was home, my mind was not. My exaggerated sense of responsibility was interfering with my relationship to my husband and daughters. Finally Barry requested that I resign from some committees. Torn between my sense of responsibility and love for my family, I came to realize the need for moderation in all things. Thus I did resign from some activities. It was a major decision to moderate service to our faith in order to preserve the happiness and well-being of our family, but it gave us more time to secure a spiritually rich and happy environment for our children.
>
> A later turning point was when Barry was traveling extensively for work while we also served in a socioeconomic development project. He was meeting all kinds of interesting people and seeing new places while my routine seemed very limited. After saying many prayers for detachment, I made a conscious and firm decision to not

permit thoughts of jealousy or distrust to enter my mind. I knew that if I did, it would be a cancer that would destroy the fulfilling and beautiful relationship that we had developed.

On one hand, Marilyn and Barry's story would appear to have required significant sacrifice on Marilyn's part. This is certainly true if one regards homemaking as a demeaning role. The Bahá'í writings also affirm a principle that tends to be forgotten in social rhetoric—that the station of mothering is valued and significant. According to Bahá'í writings, there is "no nobler deed."[4] This is not a mandate for keeping women "stuck" in the home. The critical element is choice. Bahá'í families are meant to be consultative, and the process by which they arrive at decisions is collaborative.

The Influence of Family

The Rhodys offered a perspective on how our own childhoods and experiences with our parents can shape our perceptions of marriage. Marilee shared the following: "My own childhood definitely affected my expectations and perceptions of marriage—I was fortunate to be born into a very loving family, and my parents were devoted Christians who consciously served God and humanity and were adoring of all of us and of one another all their lives. (They were also the only sexual partners they both had all their lives.) I, therefore, expected to have a happy and successful marriage and would not consider any other possibility! Our childhood experiences of family relations were quite different."

David Rhody explained, "My parents, on the other hand, did not have a very loving relationship, although they always remained together when others did not. Overt affection was not common as I grew up, and I have been affected by this all my life. I still find it difficult to demonstrate my feelings after all these years of marriage."

Ahkivgak Kiana wrote about the importance of family influence:

> I had parents who were married when they were about twenty years old, and they are now old geezers (I mean elderly, as in sixties). They are still married and poking fun at each other. Without getting into the lengthy family history, I suppose it is fair to say that my parents' and grandparents' ability to remain together was very much due to the fact that Bahá'í laws safeguarded them from common pitfalls, and Bahá'í guidance assisted them in attempting to live in contradiction to the greater social forces continually attempting to subvert and corrupt every principle they clung to and every law they followed.

Ahkivgak confirmed a theme which has run throughout all of these stories: that respect is paramount, and that parents and grandparents provide a great deal of influence and modeling in marriages. Marriage is a process, and society can and will undermine it, but a principled, spiritual belief system can provide people with a strong grounding in what they want to achieve together.

Keeping a Healthy Distance
with Family

All couples rely to some degree on feedback from close friends and family in times of difficulty. I asked Andrea and Steve Doran if they had any advice they wanted to offer for this book. Andrea and Steve have five children and one small, adored granddaughter. For long periods of their marriage, they have lived in northern Canada. There can be a sense of isolation in some of these postings, through the long winters, and as Steve works in the medical profession, their family has seen some of the stresses that can arise in different situations. Steve noted that distance from family could either be helpful or very difficult. He said,

> I attribute much of the success of our marriage to the fact that we have lived apart from each others' families. I can't say enough about this. Of course we are cognizant that we probably missed many great opportunities and resources as a result. These are things such as family support, encouragement, wisdom, experiences, and so on. However, on the other hand, we have learned to depend on each other more and pull through some hard times because of this simple fact. Growth comes through tests, and not having the traditional support system of extended family certainly makes the tests more difficult and the marriage stronger.

Steve added some further thoughts: "The first decade of our married life was spent in relatively isolated places. In many of these places we could have been, for all intents and purposes, living in a cabin in the woods. We had a lot of interaction with the people native to the area, but we shared very little cultural or traditional values with them. We were isolated."

When Steve and Andrea speak of this isolation, they are talking about some of the northernmost communities in Canada. They have lived in Rankin Inlet, Moose Factory, Iqaluit, and the Yukon; in the latter, Andrea told me, they were so isolated that they had to drive an hour and a half to get gas, and in order to get groceries, she would sometimes call the social worker with her grocery list and get the groceries brought once a week.

Steve noted, "There's something to be said about sharing time among people with the same background. Immerse yourself into another culture and see if this is not so. Sometimes we really missed access to those parts of our lives we had left behind. We gave a lot up to serve our Faith and for the adventure of traveling through unknown territory."

He added, however, "During these years we never truly felt alone, not in the true sense of the word. Yes, we were no longer surrounded by familiar things that we had known all our lives, and we felt the absence of stimulating conversation with people from the same educational and cultural roots. However, we still had each other, our children, and our faith. These things remained intact even though we were no longer a part of the society of people that had given them to us."

They learned a great deal about living in another culture, a process that increased their reliance on one another—more, perhaps, than remaining in the cities would have done.

Steve continued, "We did everything together—everything. We spent lots of time doing things together. I'm using that 'together' word a lot because I believe that's the key element to our successful marriage. Those were the days before VCRs, before computers, and before video games. Much of our time was taken up with outdoor pursuits such as hiking, berry picking, dog-sledding, canoeing, skiing, and building things. We were very active in a physical sense and very healthy as a result."

Andrea and Steve shared a photograph with me from their time in the north. She is wearing an "amounti," carrying a small child cuddled near the fur of its oversized hood, warmly against her back, and she is standing, smiling, in the bright winter sun, surrounded by snowdrifts shoulder-deep. She seems warm and comfortable in temperatures some forty below Celsius, and their dog Muff is standing at her knee, taking a rest from hauling her groceries on a sled.

Steve shared more of their story: "Evenings were a time of creativity—reading, writing letters, writing stories, and playing family games. There was always something to do, and we did it together. We fostered very strong ties and fused bonds that, like a young, developing, healthy body, have served us well for many years after we left that life behind."

Steve added, "We didn't have the blessings of family support, but neither did we have the problems of family interference either. We developed our own ways—ways that evolved from the Bahá'í writings and through our own experiences, love, and respect for each other. These bonds grew stronger with each passing day."

Sometimes, the Doran family went south, on holidays.

Steve added, "Whenever we could we went to places where we spent time with people from the same backgrounds. We attended educational workshops, conferences, conventions, or simply visited people in other communities. In these settings we thrived and rejuvenated ourselves mentally, emotionally, and spiritually. These were great times, and we always returned to our pioneering post energized and 'loaded for bear.' I can recall when traveling home after these visits how we shared our thoughts, our desires, and made plans together—always together. There was never any other way but together."

Andrea noted, "You have to expect difficulties."

Steve continued, "Things were not always great in the places we lived, but our marriage was always strong, intact, and our love and loyalty for each other was never an issue. Those bonds that we developed, like that strong healthy body, continue to serve us today. The mutual love and respect is still intact. We are not without tests; this is not heaven, but we never face a test alone. We draw strength from one another, and are still 'loaded for bear.'"

Andrea shared her view of these times, adding, "There will be times when one's behavior is in line with the Bahá'í teachings. At other times, one or the other, or both, will be struggling to behave in accordance with the teachings. When this happens, there are choices to be made. Many of us seek the advice of friends or family. This practice, however, may make things worse as it is easy to cross the line of what is advice and what is backbiting. Once something has entered into the public arena you will find that you still need to find a solution that works for both the marriage partners, but this may be more complicated if somehow you feel a need to justify the decision for those with whom you have consulted."

Andrea clarified by explaining that she and Steve had used the resource available to Bahá'ís, which is the Local Spiritual Assembly. This is a group of nine Bahá'ís who are elected each year in communities where there are nine or more adult Bahá'ís. In addition to ensuring the smooth functioning of the Bahá'ís in the locale, the Assembly provides a place for consulting in an absolutely confidential manner. In any marriage, there are only two people. What happens when deadlock occurs? For Bahá'ís who choose to trust the Assembly, there is the freedom to ask for advice and to know that the advice will remain private. This is done in a prayerful and loving manner. As Andrea expressed it, "I think those times of challenge should be kept private. Or, a person can go to the Local Spiritual Assembly and use it. Don't put family and friends in a position to judge you or your marriage. Write it all down for the Spiritual Assembly, and ask for their input."

She explained that at one point in their lives, she had felt a need for such spiritual guidance. She noted, "Of course Steve and I love one another. But there can be complicating factors. You need to be prepared, if you go to an Assembly, to listen to its advice." They described the experience of consulting with the Assembly as "one of the most precious experiences of our lives."

Of consultation with the Spiritual Assembly, she observed, "They gave us love, advice based on the writings of the faith, and we grew stronger, both as individuals and as a couple."

Andrea continued, "I was then, and still am, comforted by the thought that I should do what my Assembly has advised. I can be free from the doubts, and second thoughts, that so often accompany a person when a decision is acted upon but there is not really an apparent win-win scenario. Sometimes life is just difficult, and the freedom of having relied on God, and the advice from the Assembly, is very liberating. It also allows you to direct your energies forward toward growth and not waste it on guilt or recriminations."

She acknowledged that other people can have different experiences with situations where they consult a Spiritual Assembly, but for her and for Steve, it had been a wonderful experience and had assisted them through some challenging times.

I was interested that Steve had emphasized the isolation that had created such togetherness and that Andrea had noted that their love was never in question. Both spoke about their reliance on one another and about how their faith and family created deep bonds. A romantic view of love would suggest that "love conquers all." The picture that was emerging from these narratives was that love was a contributing factor to the sustenance of the marriages but that consultation, respect, and patience were required for the marriage to develop. Steve and Andrea have been married happily since 1977, and they continue to enjoy serving their faith and family, together.

The Support of Family

Another couple shared their story of perseverance through what appeared to be almost impossible odds. Arnold and his wife Junia are struggling with their marriage after almost two decades. Part of their struggle involves overwhelming challenges with health issues: both Junia and their son Calixte are HIV positive as a result of infection from Junia's first husband. Also, after many years of marriage, Junia became a "born again" Christian, so that she and Arnold, who has been a Bahá'í since the 1970s, have very different views of spirituality. I asked Arnold how it helped him to be able to consult his parents.

Arnold says that when they learned of Junia's illness during her pregnancy with Calixte, they both said, "God has given us this child, and we will be content with the will of God. If He takes him back, we will yield him with open arms." There were many, many tears. Arnold attributes the support of his family, and especially the values learned from his parents, for the strength to continue. Arnold is the eldest son of a French Canadian Catholic family, and of the seven children of Emile and Bibiane Perreault, six chose the Bahá'í Faith. Arnold kindly interviewed his parents, Emile and Bibiane, about the success of their marriage of more than sixty years, and I had several conversations with them in the summer of 2005.

Emile and Bibianne Perreault, who have been married sixty years, are in their mid-eighties. They summarized the most important spiritual principle in the long years of their marriage as "patience." Their Catholic faith is very important to them, and their family of seven children is very close. They attribute the success of their marriage very simply to the fact that "we love each other," and have evolved what they call "teamwork" when it comes to taking care of their family. They have farmed in Saskatchewan for most of their lives, and they have found that an equitable division of tasks served them well. They came to count on each other and "trust each other's better judgment" in consulting. They do have different styles of dealing with emotions: according to Arnold, Bibiane tends to keep her feelings to herself, while Emile, normally a fairly voluble man, will become silent for a while. They do not place much importance on these small areas, however. Their lifelong goal has been to work hard to provide for their family.

They understand the importance of sacrifice, having lived through the Depression years and the Second World War. What they note is that they don't think about the marriage itself so much; they just keep busy. When they are working hard, any differences that arise just aren't a "big deal." They noted that their own respective childhoods had been a preparation for marriage: they expected to be married, and they expected the marriage to endure and be happy. Today, they are devoted to one another. This is the model they have provided their children.

These families have demonstrated endurance, grounded in spiritual fortitude and in abiding love. They have a tenacity that is almost steely in its resolve, and like other couples, simply refuse to admit defeat. Arnold and Junia, despite cultural differences, age differences, religious disagreements, and health challenges, believe that they were destined for one another and want to stay married. They believe in marriage, and both appreciate the example offered by Arnold's parents. Arnold's sister mentioned to me that the cultural differences have been significant, and Junia told me that she has come to love many aspects of Canada but that living in an isolated community in rural Saskatchewan can also be difficult. Nonetheless, they have persevered and remained in St. Brieux, Saskatchewan.

They continue to struggle to maintain their marriage, as their religious views differ considerably, but each is committed to keeping the love for each other alive. Both Junia's and Calixte's illness take a background role, in some ways, to just living each day. Each partner functions within his or her own religious community: Arnold and their sons actively attend Bahá'í events, and Junia goes to numerous churches. Most of her friends are found in different church denominations in the area around where they live. Arnold continues to travel almost every weekend to visit with his parents, or his siblings, and sometimes Junia joins him, but mostly she prefers to attend church events rather than family gatherings. Since Junia no longer accepts the Catholicism of her childhood, and the elder Perreaults are Catholics while most of Arnold's siblings are Bahá'í, she often feels more comfortable at her church gatherings. But both soldier on in their marriage, and they have chosen to stay together and live with the devastating illness from which Junia and Calixte suffer. Their continued perseverance in the face of such overwhelming odds represents true courage in marriage, and the support of Emile and Bibiane demonstrates the strength that can come from the support of family members.

4

EXPRESSING SEXUALITY

It should not happen that upon the occurrence of a slight friction of displeasure between husband and wife, the husband would think of union with some other woman or, God forbid, the wife also think of another husband. This is contrary to the standard of heavenly value and true chastity. The friends of God must so live and conduct themselves, and evince such excellence of character and conduct, as to make others astonished. The love between husband and wife should not be purely physical, nay rather it must be spiritual and heavenly. These two souls should be considered as one soul. How difficult it would be to divide a single soul! Nay, great would be the difficulty!

'Abdu'l-Bahá

To speak about sexuality is to speak of something private. As such, I was particularly grateful that some people were willing to offer their thoughts openly. Far from being shy or embarrassed about this subject, couples offered their opinions in frank and non-judgmental terms. Many did so from an unusual standpoint: Bahá'í teachings require chastity, considering it one of the healthy foundations to marriage. There appears to be a special, added sweetness to a marriage where sexuality is a gift of the marriage and is not taken for granted. Often, couples I spoke with said that sexuality outside of marriage could be blinding. It was more difficult to see character when sexuality was involved. Sexual expression outside of marriage complicated relationships and seemed to imply a commitment which might not have occurred without physical intimacy.

It is important to understand why Bahá'ís try to follow laws regarding sexual intimacy, especially in a society where freedom in this area appears more common. Chastity in sexual expression runs counter to many of the prevailing norms and assumptions of western society, and in some cultures, chastity is only valued for men. In Bahá'í teaching, the expectation is for both women and men to be adorned with chastity, as part of the committed love of their marriage.

Reasons for Chastity Before Marriage

The essence of the reasons for chastity can be summed up in the following quotation by the Universal House of Justice: "In considering the effect of obedience to the laws on individual lives, one must remember that the purpose of this life is to prepare the soul for the next. Here one must learn to control and direct one's animal impulses, not to be a slave to them. . . . Sometimes the course may seem very hard, but one can witness, again and again, that the soul who steadfastly obeys the law of Bahá'-u'lláh, however hard it may seem, grows spiritually."[1]

The "test of chastity" is frequently discussed in this chapter, and the majority of the couples interviewed for this book are Bahá'ís who were faithful to the principles of their religion. As a result, they had not slept with one another prior to their marriage. They were, however, very honest about the power of their attraction for one another. Perhaps the most eloquent response to my questions about sexuality and its role in marriage was Don Dainty's, recalling his newly-wed status: "I couldn't believe the sublimity of it all."

David Hall sent in a lovely comment on sex. He emphasized that it was a facetious account, but I appreciated that as with all things in marriage, humor can help to view everything in a happier light. He wrote, "As to why our marriage has been so successful, I would have said it was the sex. And we are happy about it—Ann tells me we can have sex in the next world too. Even during those times when she says I am going to have to wait until the next world to have sex again she does it in such a loving way!"

Bob LeBlanc and his wife Louise had waited a year for their marriage. They noted that they believed the chastity they had practiced in the period while they were waiting to marry had been an important foundation for their marriage itself. Bob said, of chastity, "We believed in it. We had to wait. It was a big test." He noted, though, "There are gradients of chastity: like in some places I'd be looking at Louise through a veil or just at her eyes; in some places we'd hold hands, in some we kissed, but we didn't 'do it,' and we were proud of ourselves. I think there was a blessing from obeying that law that has brought a purity to our sexual relationship."

Louise agreed: "We look at the preciousness, the sacredness of sex in marriage."

Bob speculated, "What difference would it have made, if we hadn't waited?"

Louise thought out loud, "The sacredness." She laughed, "And the reward was great sex!" She continued, "No, because it is a reward. I know that there would have always been that niggling feeling of guilt if we'd done it. I also see the safety in the law. Sex can definitely blind you, and had we gone that far, I always would have wondered, was I attracted to this man for sexual reasons or for his spiritual qualities? The night of our marriage I realized that it was well worth waiting for."

Both said, of the wedding, "The sanctity of marriage was consummated."

Bob agreed, saying, "It was totally under God's blessing, it was freeing and lovely. I think kids miss out on that now."

From the stories I heard, it seemed that a steadfast commitment to chastity during courtship and a view of sexual intimacy as a sacred act almost always led to a healthy marriage. It seemed to naturally lead to passion, and I talked with several couples about the element of passion in their marriage.

The Lover and His Beloved

I asked Ali Khajavi about this specific aspect of marriage, partly because he had viewed the romantic notion of marriage as very different from his cultural perspective. I asked him about passion. He grinned and said, "I am very happy."

Ali and Tracy Khajavi have two young boys and, like many couples with small children, noted that their times for intimacy were rare. Much energy is focused in children when they are young. Passion does not disappear, but there may be less emphasis on nurturing that part of the marriage. In fact, many of the long-married couples noted that over time, sex became less important. Suzanne Schuurman explained that for her and Hubert, there were moments of humor:

Though we had planned to put off parenthood till after we were both finished studying, in the first year of our marriage I had to tell Hubert that we were expecting a baby. His immortal response was "How did it happen?" By the time Hubert graduated with the Governor General's Medal, we had two little daughters and were bursting out of our one bedroom apartment.

From the first meeting there had been a strong sexual attraction between us. We had agreed that we would follow Bahá'í laws and abide by chastity until marriage. Often before we were married we included the only other Bahá'í in our town of St. John's—Bruce Matthew—in our activities, as an effective chaperone.

My first inclination was to skim over this aspect of married life partly, I think because our culture is saturated with a prurient interest in sex. I had always felt that the interaction between the lover and the beloved constituted a metaphor for our relationship to God. The ecstasy on the paintings and statues of saints made the connection in my mind with the rapture of intercourse. After all, when in our daily lives do we experience that kind of intensity of emotion?

When I came across this section in Bertrand Russell's autobiography, it was the first confirmation that someone else held the same idea. The section reads, "I have sought love, first because it brings ecstasy—ecstasy so great that I would often have sacrificed all the rest of life for a few hours of this joy. I have sought it next because it relieves loneliness—that terrible loneliness in which one shivering consciousness looks over the rim of the world into the cold unfathomable lifeless abyss. I have sought it finally, because in the union of love I have seen, in a mystic miniature, the prefiguring vision of the heaven that saints and poets have imagined."[3]

Later, when reading the first volume of *The Revelation of Bahá'u'lláh* by Adib Taherzadeh, I was thrilled to read in the introduction, "All created things, whether tangible or intangible, come into being as a result of the intercourse between two elements which assume the function of male and female. This pattern is followed throughout the whole of creation and the birth of religion is no exception." Here was a paradigm for the sexual expression of love in marriage that held infinite possibilities for learning of spiritual realities. With time I grew increasingly grateful to God for having given us this doorway to understanding. As a teenager, when I had read Bahá'u'lláh's words on the "true seeker," some passages had puzzled me, such as this one: "He must so cleanse his heart that no remnant of either love or hate may linger therein, lest that love blindly incline him to error."[4]

If love was good why could it also "incline to error"? Only with time could I see the wisdom and truth of this verse and begin to understand another verse that reads, "Only when the lamp of search, of earnest striving, of longing desire, of passionate devotion, of fervid love, of rapture, and ecstasy, is kindled within the seeker's heart, and the breeze of His loving-kindness is wafted upon his soul, will . . . the lights of knowledge and certitude envelop his being."[5]

As a young Bahá'í my "lamp of search" had been lit, but it was in marriage that I learned about fervid love, rapture, and ecstasy, and from that I was able to extrapolate the kind of intensity possible in my love for God.

Sex as a Spiritual Act

The intense love to which Suzanne refers here creates an analogy with which other couples tended to agree. The love for the other, and the attraction for the other, appears to be grounded in terms which are not simply physical. When love also has a spiritual element, sexual expression becomes more spiritual, in some mysterious way.

This spiritual power of attraction seems to allow couples to take pleasures in the small things. Ron Nablo described his feelings during his courtship of Edna:

> Edna and I have often told the story of how we met and the romantic events that followed. Some came soon and some much later. . . . I first saw her at a party . . . and she happened to be singing a duet . . . I was awed both by her beauty and the loveliness of her voice, and I did not give a thought to pursuing her at that time, as I simply thought that I would not have a chance.
>
> But, later on . . . in 1953 . . . it was a different matter. She was alone and on her way to dinner with friends, and I set out in pursuit, and I made sure I sat beside her at dinner. That was the year we all attended a Bahá'í conference in Chicago. Edna went by train with many other Bahá'ís, but I hitchhiked. I found the train, met Edna, grabbed her suitcase and proceeded to carry it to the YWCA where she was staying. I ended up carrying it one full block more than necessary because of turning the wrong way. Funny how you find out the hard way that a person's sense of direction is almost absolute zero. Of course, not having a good sense of direction is not and

never was a reason not to marry someone, but I might have been warned about many a lost mile had I known of it! Edna and I stayed very close at the conference, sitting together at all events. I picked her up every morning and went for walks at night after the events. . . . One night we were walking down the Michigan waterfront, hand in hand, when suddenly there was a swishing sound, and Edna literally leaped into my arms. It was just the water coming up a pipe, but she thought it was a snake. She was very embarrassed. I was very delighted.

A Healthy Sex Life

While sexual attraction is clearly important in the early days of a relationship, almost all the couples expressed a variation on the theme articulated by June Barrow: "It's important in the beginning, because it is part of the spark that causes you to come together and make a commitment, but as time goes on, you realize that it's not as important as you may have thought."

Marilyn Smith concurred. She said, "It seems more important early in marriage because it is a natural thing and contributes to the creation of new souls. . . . It is enjoyable and provides a special bond or relationship shared with only one person."

Ron Nablo made an interesting comment about this uniqueness of the beloved person. He said:

Having talked about the beginning of things with Edna and me, I can also say that I loved her from Day 1 of meeting her, in the romantic sense. I also underestimated her. I had seen some evidence of her talent in music and art, but I had little firsthand knowledge of it. I also knew nothing of her keen mind, wisdom, understanding, thoughtfulness, mature judgment—far beyond her years—and her talent for raising children. I only found out her capacity for sharing life fully with me by marrying her, not by simply having thoughts about such things. I don't know how young men should be taught what to look for in a wife, but they should not be allowed to seek their brides using the ridiculous dating tools that society offers. I never did use nightclubs to meet anyone, but so many people do. I also think dances are wholly inadequate for the young men who are shy and inept.

Maury Miloff offered a similar perspective on his first attraction to Helen. He said, "Our selection of each other came after quite a bit of prayer; getting that right probably saves a few battles—although, perhaps I overstate things since meeting Helen was like a bolt of lightning for me (coming, mind you, after months of arduous prayer for the right partner), which I still don't completely understand. I was amazed at how quickly I became sure she was the right one for me—perhaps my soul was intuiting something beyond the normal senses."

Tracy Khajavi noted the success of a romantic gesture:

A friend said when he had met me for the first time that 'he had a guy for me.' Of course I didn't think anything of it, as people were always trying to fix up single people. When Ali phoned for the first time, I also didn't think too much of it. Then there was an event held out of town, and volunteers were needed to help set it up. We found that we were both volunteering the same day . . . so we met up with each other and talked all day as we worked. We talked about all sorts of stuff, but it didn't seem to Ali like I was all that interested in him. So he thought he'd better do something quick. He soon invited me for a coffee. I said I'd try to make it (I was working or something). When I showed up he had bought me twenty-four roses, which floored me. I had never had someone buy me flowers before going out for some coffee. This finally got the reaction he was looking for. We played with the idea of marriage, and after a dinner he cooked for me and my mom (as is the culture in Iran), I figured I'd be a fool to not marry the guy. Once we made our decision, we got married three weeks later.

The character of an individual is an important theme in exploring the role of intimacy in marriage. All the couples referred to the power of attraction, but some expressed this in an intriguing manner.

Sylvia de Vasquez said,

I'm sure you will hear from most couples that a healthy sex life also helps a marriage, and we definitely would agree. However, I might define a healthy sex life a little differently than just having sex; I think healthiness in sex is as much the ability to talk about what's wrong between you sexually as well as how much you enjoy each other. I won't go into personal detail, but perhaps now I'm speaking as a reasonably chaste former Bahá'í youth: a healthy sex life is as much about honest communication about sex as it is about having sex. I used to think that once we were married, sex would just be an all-the-time thing that my husband and I would enjoy. I learned that while sex is important, it isn't important enough to have it all the time.

Love Versus Sex

Peter Brady was quite expressive about the sexual relationship that he and Muguette enjoyed after many years of marriage: "Sex is very important, but it is not the ultimate goal of marriage. It is part of marriage—the most intimate way to show and share our feelings for our spouses. Holding hands, even in our sixties, is enjoyable. Kissing each other in public, a caress or squeeze of the shoulder or hand, is still part of our love life. These are as important as making love; they can be part of the prelude or just a sign of our affection."

Peter made an important distinction:

We make love; having sex is an unthinking, egocentric act of two people who do not care about their partner's needs and desires. To make love is to ensure that other person is also satisfied and happy. The purpose of making love, above and beyond producing children, is the most intimate way of demonstrating my love for my wife.

The time for making love is also important. If either of us is feeling tired, irritable, or bothered by a problem, we do not try to make love. . . . On occasion, we have talked and consulted rather than make love at that time. I look forward to making love to my wife and dream of doing so. Through our married life we have learned what pleases our partner, not just ourselves.

Likewise, laughter and silly jokes are as important as the physical aspect. These can break unrealized tension and relax us or become part of the games we play. My wife says I have impeccable timing and often catch her off guard with a remark, or the way I will say something.

As a woman, I was very much struck with the idea that a husband might "dream" of making love to his wife. It seemed to be a very lovely image. Peter's wife Muguette noted, a bit more shyly, "There again I share everything he has said. I would like to be able to make him laugh as much as he makes me laugh, but my sense of humor is different. I find that I am less funny than he is with his jokes. He is more able to make things humorous."

Peter noted, however, that Muguette's demonstrative nature was part of their initial attraction. He said,

When we met, she automatically took my arm even before I offered it. It was a very simple, straightforward, and natural gesture. Later when we walked to a restaurant we held hands. It too felt natural and comfortable. There was no awkwardness about it, there were none of the usual mental games I usually played, trying to guess what my date wanted me to do or say. We talked like two people who had known each other all our lives.

It was so clearly different from my previous few but thoroughly disastrous dating experiences. There was no

feeling of expectation, no need to pretend to be something other than what we were. Even now, neither of us is
good at playing games with each other. What you see is
basically what we are.

Within a week I told her I loved her, and within two
weeks of our first date, we were engaged.

Finding Intimacy

Cheryl and Gordon Epp had an experience different from
those expressed by other couples in the development of the
sexuality in their marriage. Having just turned eighteen,
Cheryl Kinchen married Gordon Epp, who was twenty-one.
Cheryl tells me that unlike many of the other couples who
have spoken about this subject and who have said that sex
became less important over time, for her and Gord, it has
become more important. She explained,

> I made a transition from struggling with intimacy in a
> physical relationship to believing in it and enjoying it as a
> normal part of life.
>
> I stopped "fearing love" and started to feel passion for
> my life and passion for my spiritual helpmate. Some of
> the transition was gradual, over time, and some of it was
> sudden, through a particular experience. For example, just
> before our twenty-fifth anniversary, we were planning an
> elaborate celebration, and I was preparing to write a love
> song for Gord while he was working nights. I was sitting
> in front of the fireplace with the lights down low, listen-
> ing to Sarah McLachlan over and over, absorbed in her

words. The "night was my companion," I let myself "shed a tear" and "feel a rage," and I didn't want to "spend forever here and not be satisfied."[6]

After the anniversary celebration, for the first time in twenty-five years of marriage, we spent a three-day weekend alone in a romantic hotel suite. I didn't know what I had been missing until I experienced it. . . . Three days of focusing on our relationship was enough to get past some of the psychological barriers and feel the relaxing benefits of a spiritual and physical union. Here, it was just my husband and me on the same wavelength. We had spent so much time parenting together, we were more aware of our differences.

She commented that she didn't know how Gord had been so patient in the first years of their marriage, and she suggested that I ask him about that. I did.

He laughed and said, "I don't know if I was always that patient!" Then he paused to reflect and noted,

I tried to be. . . . I didn't have clear expectations of what it should be; I didn't know what was realistic to expect from another person. The question implies that I had reason to be impatient, and really I was learning as I went along. We're quite different in nature, so I suppose it's not surprising that it was reflected in our sexuality.

I had to struggle with the fact that Cheryl's lack of expressiveness, which had an effect on our intimacy, might not change. I got the feeling that she loved me, but I had to accept that she might not be able to love me back the way I would have liked her to. But there were other supportive things about our relationship that made me not want to give up on it. We always had a friendship and there was always effort and growth made on both of our parts, so it was worth maintaining.

The couple agreed that there were important changes over time that had contributed to the unity they now feel. Cheryl spoke in particular of the counseling she had been able to experience after the death of their second child. I should note here that Gord and Cheryl have endured what is probably the most painful tragedy in life that anyone could imagine: of the three boys born to them, two were diagnosed with muscular dystrophy. Their second, Salim, died at age eleven, and their son Angus, now nineteen, requires 100% of their care and attention.

Gord is a stay-at-home caregiver, of whom Cheryl said, with a great deal of tenderness in her voice, "The kind of things Gord has gone through have changed him: he's a caregiver, for Angus and for me. If we hadn't had two boys with MD, that may not have happened."

Cheryl's own changes she attributes, in part, to changes within herself through the counseling that had to occur before she could deal with the loss of her son. She said,

Gord and my mother are very emotionally expressive, and I always somehow thought they were right to be so emotional, and I was wrong to not express my emotions as freely. I was feeling inadequate and unaware that it's just a way of being. I had to learn that I could be less outwardly expressive and still show emotion. There was nothing wrong with not showing emotions outwardly, but I had to let people around me know something about what was going on. For example, my mom gets all teary-eyed when we say goodbye at the airport, and I am always calmer about it. So I learned to respond in some way rather than not at all, and I would phone her when she got home and talk to her about it. Some people have trouble crying in front of other people, but they do cry.

I realized I could tell my husband that I needed time to think about something before responding. I got to choose how and when I was going to respond; it was empowering.

She spoke quite a bit about the level of discovery of herself, and then she told me about an important experience.

"At a certain point of the grief counseling, I wrote a goodbye letter to Salim, and then on my own, as an extension of this, I wrote a letter from him to me because I needed to hear from him. I just let the thoughts flow freely. He told me to take the time that I would have given to him and give it to his brothers and his father, like a gift from him. It was a way of honoring him."

Now she finds herself reflecting on her own experience with marriage by watching her eldest son and his wife develop their relationship together. She said, "Our marriage being successful has something to do with being patient and persistent and with letting each person be who they are and blossom in his or her own way. As long as both individuals are growing, there's hope."

Loyalty to One's Partner in Marriage

The Bahá'í teaching of chastity before marriage also implies absolute loyalty to one's partner during marriage. Shoghi Effendi, the Guardian of the Bahá'í Faith, wrote to an individual Bahá'í, "The question you raise as to the place in one's life that a deep bond of love with someone we meet other than our husband or wife can have is easily defined in view of the teachings. Chastity implies both before and after marriage an unsullied, chaste sex life. Before marriage absolutely chaste, after marriage absolutely faithful to one's chosen companion. Faithful in all sexual acts, faithful in word and in deed."[7]

It is not an easy thing to keep a marriage intact. Several passages from the Bahá'í writings, like the one by Shoghi Effendi above, speak to the importance of loyalty in marriage. In fact, every faith emphasizes this quality. One of the people with whom I conversed on the subject, Steve Doran, made an interesting distinction.

He said he could understand unfaithfulness. It was no surprise when, at one point or another, one of the partners might make an error of judgment and slip into the passion of a misjudged moment. To resist this temptation was an element of a mature character.

Yet Steve said that while a temporary unfaithfulness was grievous and saddening, it was not a loss of loyalty in the grander sense. Loyalty meant not just loyalty to one's spouse—it meant loyalty to one's faith, family, society, and to the future generations of the family that would follow. It meant, in the moment of temptation, realizing that it was not simply one's own personal satisfaction that was at stake, but an entire system that hinged on loyalty, the ability to trust, and the ability to set an example to children.

Unfaithfulness was a temporary aberration of selfishness; loss of loyalty was a lack of responsibility to future generations. Unfaithfulness might be a forgivable sin, but lack of loyalty was not for just one person to forgive—it was something that future generations would have to cope with and endure. He thought that perhaps, if people understood this, they would be less inclined to stray because they would understand that the short-term implications were outweighed by the long-term resonances of their actions. One act could create a ripple in a pond that would carry far beyond its immediate appearance.

For Steve, a key element to loyalty to one's spouse was the virtue of detachment. Here is what he had to say:

> Falling in love with another is a natural thing. In my father-in-law's words, there are thousands of people we could marry and have a great life with. I've met some very wonderful women over the years but I choose to remain loyal to my wife, and when I think of my friends that have chosen the other way and witness the tragic consequences of their decisions, it galvanizes me to stay firm in my faith and motivates me to pray for detachment.
>
> I bought a tape from Amazon of a concert of Peter, Paul, and Mary. At one point in the concert Paul stood alone on stage and did his comedy act. He spoke of when he was a young man and there was a magazine called *Life*.

This magazine included everything. Then a few years later another magazine made its debut and it was called *People*. He stood on stage and said that people are a very large part of life, that's true, but now (he indicated with his hands outstretched and moved them closer together) indicating how "people" were really a much smaller part of life. The magazine catered to a much more growing self-awareness, or was it self-centeredness? Then he said there came a magazine called *Us*, and his hands moved closer together. "There's us and there's them." So he said there would soon be a magazine called *Me*, with pages of aluminum foil where people could look at themselves and smile back at their own images. He then went on through his act imitating people who had become focused on themselves and justified their acts with "I'm being truthful to myself."

Well, I don't peruse the magazine section of bookstores, but because my brother Dave's work was being featured in one, I went in search of it and came across the magazine called *Self.* That's not *Me*, but "Self" is a pretty close runner-up!

I admire my father-in-law, who is the most unselfish person I know. I mean he doesn't even comb his hair, what's left of it. He could care less. He has been an example for me of how a person should try to live a life of service to others. He doesn't waste time concerned with himself. He's detached—I mean in the extreme. Yes, he likes his creature comforts, his digital camera, and his laptop, but that's not, in my opinion, overly materialistic. After all, God does want us to partake of the riches of the earth. Not to do so in my opinion is throwing these gifts back into God's face. Which is the greater sin? But there has to be detachment and paying attention to the real things in life.

Detachment, then, has become a fixation for me for a long time, predominating in my thoughts, when I think of all the marriages that have broken up.

I'm not a great man, and I'm not blowing my horn. These are tests, and we are told that God will not test us beyond our capacity.[2] So the thing I think is important to mention is detachment. It seems like such a vital piece of the puzzle, does it not? To surrender one's desires for the good of others would have salvaged so many of these failed marriages.

I thought Steve had raised many good points. Focusing on detachment from the petty, selfish desires that sometimes arise as tests for us during marriage can lead us to discover the things that really are important to us, such as the love for our spouse and our family. It seemed, from the stories I heard, that a natural outgrowth of loyalty to one's spouse was the feeling of commitment.

Commenting on the idea of commitment, Canadian Sylvia de Vasquez wrote of a conversation between herself and her Honduran husband, Yovanny: "We talked about what commitment means. If you enter into a marriage thinking there is a possibility that it won't work, you're doomed from the start. It is hard to explain this, but it simply never occurs to either Yovanny or me that we will ever separate. Why think about it? We're married. We work things out as a unit. Period."

Carol and David Bowie offered a similar perspective. Married at a young age as Christians, they attributed their accep-

tance of the Bahá'í teachings—which emphasize the importance of commitment to one's spouse—as important to the
unity of their marriage. They recently celebrated their fiftieth
wedding anniversary and shared the following:

David and I had our fiftieth wedding anniversary in
February 2005. Where did the time go? Well, we moved
all over the province of Ontario during the first thirty-
five years, with David's work with Ontario Hydro. At
the time of his retirement we had two children in the
next world and four in this one, including an adopted
daughter. During our first year we learned about the
Bahá'í Faith, and during the second we became Bahá'ís.
Another whole story!

Although we did not know about the Faith when we
met, we "accidentally" became very good friends during
our early weeks. We discovered there was more than just
friendship happening; David proposed and I accepted.
David asked my parents for permission to marry me. I was
sixteen and David was twenty-one when we became engaged, and eleven months later we married in Niagara Falls.
As it happened my father had to come with us to give his
approval to the marriage license application because I was
under eighteen. But we didn't realize that this would be
necessary when permission was originally sought.

In the months leading up to the wedding we decided
what turned out to be a very important thing—for both
of us, divorce was not an option. It was not something
imposed by any external affiliation, but the establishment
of what we now know as a covenant between us.

The idea of a marriage as a "covenant" seemed meaning-ful. As Wendy James succinctly put the matter, "Make sure anyone you marry can keep their promises."

Reinforcing the theme of commitment, Margaret Bremner noted that marriage requires preparation, and she commented on the importance of family example:

> I think a long-lasting marriage starts well before the marriage ceremony. Family history is a big factor. I believe that research has shown that if one's parents have divorced, one is more likely to divorce. So perhaps people coming from divorced parents may need to work harder at staying together? Both my parents and my husband's have been married for forty-some years. I think that if one goes into marriage thinking "I can always get divorced," perhaps that is more likely to happen. But if one goes into mar-riage assuming "This is for a long time, the rest of my life, forever," there is an expectation of working through tough times, putting up with things, and offering support.

This attitude was one that ran through all the narratives of the couples who contributed to this book. Almost every-one acknowledged that expecting to work through tough times, and expecting that tough times would inevitably oc-cur, was part of the reason for the happiness of their mar-riages.

Tracy Khajavi, married to an Iranian who had a strong and traditional Muslim background, met her husband Ali in Canada during a time when he was investigating and then accepting the teachings of Bahá'u'lláh. When asked about the success of her marriage to Ali, Tracy answered simply, "I think it's because we made a decision to go through life together. Sometimes it's hard, sometimes it's easy. It's a choice that we both uphold."

When asked why their marriage worked, Gordon Epp answered, "First and foremost because we love each other and are committed to each other. We've discovered this. Our hopes, expectations, and dreams are closely aligned, and it makes it easier. There is mutual supportiveness. At a certain point I learned to love Cheryl more for who she is rather than for who she might become. I still have to remind myself that I am always responsible for my own feelings and actions."

Commitment, for these couples, seemed to be inextricably linked to their love for one another, and their love for one another connected intimately to their passion for one another. The more they knew one another, the more they loved, and the more they loved, the more they were given the gift of desire. Physical intimacy was thus a form of the spiritual blessings of marriage.

5

CHILDREN

And when God gives you sweet and lovely children,
consecrate yourselves to their instruction and guidance,
so that they may become imperishable flowers
of the divine rose-garden, nightingales
of the ideal paradise, servants of the world
of humanity, and the fruit
of the tree of your life.

Attributed to 'Abdu'l-Bahá

The arrival of the first child is often a joyously anticipated event for a new family. In other cases, families come with children who are "ready-made" from previous marriages. The couples who shared their thoughts on the role of children in their lives noted, among other factors, that raising a family can be a very unifying experience.

Finding One's Own Space with Children

Some couples noted that there is a challenge in finding the right balance between independence and togetherness. Maury Miloff noted the role children can play in requiring a couple to find their way to unity: "I think we were incredible during the child-raising stage—maybe because we loved kids so much and had such a strong sense of responsibility. I suppose having similar priorities and being able to sacrifice personal interests in favor of religion, family, and community was the foundation."

Tracy Khajavi thinks her children are the most important binding force for her and for her husband: "They are the reason we do almost everything in life. Most of our thoughts revolve around them."

David and Marilee Rhody, whose marriage is strong after twenty-eight years despite having endured lengthy separations of up to three years while David was in Africa, noted how important the balance between children and personal independence was.

Marilee said, "We love one another and enjoy one another's company; we have certain interests that are different and that we encourage the other to do, but we also enjoy and participate in a number of common interests. Some are recently acquired interests while others are long-standing ones, such as bird watching, walking, working in the garden, jazz, opera, books, and so on."

David commented, "I would agree with Marilee but emphasize that we each have certain pastimes or hobbies that we feel happy doing alone. Our likes and activities intersect a lot, but we go our separate ways sometimes, and it feels fine to do that."

They noted, however, that this independence is more pronounced now that their children are grown and have left home. Life is different when the children are young. As David explained, "When the children were smaller, much of our energy was directed toward them and not to each other. This has changed to some extent now that the children are no longer living at home."

Ovidio Gomez also noted the importance of independence within the family, especially after children have entered the picture: "I think it's also important when a couple gets married that they become as one spiritually but that they don't lose their individuality. You keep your friends, and each of you spends time with them. Coral didn't like some of my friends, but she respected me and allowed me to go out with them, and I do the same for her."

The Barrows, too, commented on the effect of children in their lives. In their family, Reggie had already had children—almost grown—from his previous marriage. When asked, "How have children affected your relationship," June's answer was fairly lengthy:

They have been both a great reward and blessing as well as a twenty-year project—our adopted child is a different type of challenge, giving us experiences and challenges we didn't have with the older two boys. For example, when she didn't like a "no" answer to something, she would always threaten to leave us or else say that we weren't her "real" parents anyway and that she didn't have to respect us. In contrast, the boys never showed that particular behavior. Reg also has four children, from his previous marriage, who are almost as old as I am. His eldest daughter is forty-nine, and I'm fifty-four—he was seventeen when she was born, so now he has great-grandchildren who are teenagers and grandchildren who are as old as our children Adam and Isaac. Reg's children from his past marriage have also been a challenge in terms of working on family unity, although they never actually lived with us for more than nine months of our marriage. During our first year of marriage, Reg's eldest daughter, her four children, and her partner all lived in the same house with us. They were having a rough time, and we were trying to help them out—we didn't have our own kids yet at that time, and her kids referred to me as "grandmom" or "Aunt June." It was good training for me to work out the relationship of being a stepparent, although I didn't really have to do too much because the kids were not there much of the time, other than those first nine months.

For me, I would say that raising children has been the area where we had the most disagreements. I always felt Reg was too strict, and he felt I was too lenient. He was more old-fashioned and also had a hard time just being at ease with parenting, and I think a lot of that was due to the fact that he was extremely upset about his own parents' divorce. They divorced when he was only seven, and he had no real role model for what it meant to be a father. In spite of it all, our kids turned out pretty well, but I always attribute that to their own inner qualities and strengths rather than anything we did as parents. I would say that becoming a parent is one of the single most important things in terms of spiritual growth, in that you are literally forced to put others before yourself, and this is a good thing.

Greg and Ginny Kintz shared this same perspective about the importance of their children to the development of their marriage:

Our children have strengthened our relationship considerably because they forced us to develop many positive habits. Our practice of consultation was really refined over many child-rearing discussions. The courtesy with which we treat each other was exaggerated originally as a model for our children, but it has now become habit. We have often had youth or others spend a day with us and remark on how courteous we are to each other—even doing mundane things like laundry or going to the beach. The remarks always surprise us because it is so much a part of who we are that we forget that it is not like that for other people. Raising two daughters also helped us really come to grips with issues around equality of men and women. We wanted our marriage to be a model for our daughters of a healthy, balanced relationship.

Stuart North, who with his wife Adelie left Canada to live in Haiti, shared these thoughts about the effects of children on their relationship:

Having children has been a joy to both of us, but at the same time it has brought out the weaknesses in our marriage. When we were overseas, the demands of our faith and a full-time job made it impossible for me to be fully involved in the lives of my children. My wife was also busy with a full-time job, her service to the Faith, and the children. I was away almost every weekend, either at meetings or on teaching trips. My wife shouldered the primary responsibility for raising the children. She felt abandoned by her husband and cut off from her extended family back in Canada. This made her feel very resentful and affected her health. She did not feel that her needs or the needs of our children were being met. I, as her husband, was quite stressed much of the time. This put a great strain on our relationship. We served at our pioneer post for twelve years, and then political circumstances forced us to return to Canada. It has taken about ten years to repair, to a reasonable degree, our relationship.

Children and Grandchildren as a New Cycle in Marriage

I found it very interesting that so many couples spoke, in different ways, of cycles in their marriages. For those who had been married a long time—like the Norths, now at thirty-three years of marriage—the time and patience needed to "repair" their relationships were a necessary part of the marriage. Stuart noted significant changes, over time, and one of the significant changes in his attitude came about because of grandchildren. After having grandchildren, he said, "I mellowed out and have become more family-orientated. I enjoy being with my grandchildren very much, and I am more patient and tolerant than I was as a father. I am more sensitive to the needs of others. The burning zeal that I had to change the world overnight has been tempered by the realization that I am a very insignificant cog in a very large wheel."

Stuart also felt that having grandchildren had allowed him to become more sensitive to his wife's differences: "I am very careful what I say to my wife since I have learned over the years that we have a very different sense of humor and approach to life. We are very polite with each other and show our affection with occasional hugs."

Rick Gordon also talked about how children had impacted his marriage. He said, "Our marriage has followed a kind of bell curve, relatively smooth at the beginning and end, with a serious learning curve in between. Critical changes in our marriage have divided our time together into three stages: (1) B.C. (before children), (2) H.C. (having children, which was the roller coaster ride of our lives), (3) A.D. (after departure—from my employment). These stages could be characterized as (1) peaceful, (2) frenetic, (3) peaceful.

Another challenge, in family life, both for the spouse and for the children, is when there is an illness in the family. Reginald Barrow commented on this, with respect to June's cancer: "Since June's serious illness, I have put more value on our time together and our peaceful moments. June has always set high spiritual standards, which I have aspired to."

"I have become more tolerant, and also more self confident, as a result of Reg's constant encouragement of my abilities and talents," added June. "We also think that our relationship has actually gotten better with age, in that we've studied the writings together and tried to apply them, which is something neither one of us really did seriously before our marriage, although Reg was a third-generation Bahá'í and I was not a Bahá'í at all before we met."

Maury Miloff also shared some thoughts about the changes children bring to a marriage:

I would break down my twenty-five-year marriage into phases. The first stage of initial attraction was unproblematic. Fantastic would be a better word! The soaring love and spiritual attitudes in which we had immersed ourselves brought the joy and excitement of great promise. The few years after marriage and before children are, in my memory, marked by intense and fruitful discussion, getting to know each other, figuring out who we were and where we came from. The period of the infancy and early childhood of each of our three children were years of miracles and blessings . . . as well as exhaustion. I am not sure if it was love and sacrifice, or neglect, but while the children were still in the home and not yet at school we managed to put off and onto the back burner the whole gamut of our personal needs. Advice number one: if you can give your children the best of you, it will be worth it!

Maury noted the different stages of marriage. When the children left home, it was an important shift of perspective for the couple. As Maury expressed it:

The difficult times for us really came at so-called middle age when the ghosts of old dreams and a life unlived return home to haunt you—and there is no escape. We had achieved many of our main life goals in the areas of education, career, marriage, pioneering, children, and community service. You slow down enough to stop and ponder. The world of possibilities rolls open wide before you and there you stand, a stick figure, perhaps a caricature of a real human being, not quite on solid ground, reviewing your life and knowing that your destiny is in your own frozen or shaking palm.

I think Maury is commenting here on what is sometimes jokingly referred to as a "mid-life crisis." He noted the intense self-scrutiny which can be a part of this period: "Here is the life you made. Is it a good one? Is it enough? Does it meet your needs and fulfill your hopes? Is it really you? Here is all the life I haven't made that is still to come. What is it I want? Who am I really? Who is this person beside me? What do I really feel about her? What are we like together? It was a time of critical examination, of emotions bursting their old, no longer needed walls—not 'a kind of,' but a definite rebirth."

Such questioning can be a time both for terrible grief and for wonderful opportunity. As Maury explained, "This was for me a troubling time of ferment and anguish when I wanted, with the purity of white hot spirit, to destroy all old structures and processes. To make what was underground above ground. A time of great certainty—yes, certainty— and great confusion. And, perhaps because I was careful to not flare out of control, it lasted years. It was an emotional pressure cooker."

Maury's honesty in describing this period is something I wish to honor. He continued,

> During this period, I read voraciously, analyzed my dreams, wrote, drew, and experienced great highs and great lows. It was a time of turning towards, trying to find unity, with my own self and away from my partner. It was a time of separating and reconstituting all elements and a return-ing to who I was.
>
> A lot of painful lessons were learned on both sides, truths about ourselves. A lot of garbage, illusions, half-truths, unhelpful attitudes and behaviors, and hidden traumas were cleared away. And in its wake came, haltingly but

surely, more understanding, peace of mind, acceptance, and appreciation. Now, I feel we are just beginning a new and rewarding phase to our relationship. It's a very gradual process. The crucible is pain, but the benefits are palpable, and there is no way out.

There is, of course, a way out; when painful times come in marriages, many people choose to leave the marriage. Most of the couples who contributed to the book indicated that it was during these times of pain that their commitment was most important; patiently working out the challenges, listening to each other, and looking forward to a time when they would succeed in dealing with a particular test—rather than giving up—were critical factors in weathering the storms of marriage. Living in the moment could get disheartening; it was always necessary to keep an eye on hope for the future.

The Trials of Raising Children

Susan Eghrari Moraes spoke about how raising children offers a developmental perspective for the entire marriage and requires the ability to look to the future:

A sustainable marriage implies concern with the future, the sustaining of spiritual values in your life, happiness, or inner spiritual equilibrium. Understanding the process of the dynamics of marriage helps to broaden our optimistic vision of the upcoming challenges for the couple. After fifteen years of marriage, if we have children, this is when they are entering their adolescent stage. The couple enters into their adolescent stage as well.

A friend of ours, Luis Henrique Beust, explained in his talks about adolescents and parents that the whole family enters into the adolescent stage when the children become teenagers. During the times that children are very young, and into adolescence, they consume (like crazy). They consume material goods, energy, and time, and require constant attention and effort from their parents. Later, as they mature and branch out into adulthood, there is a more 'sustainable' time for the parents, who often segue into more material comfort as they are no longer responsible for their children financially. It is also a time when parents can enjoy more time together, less interruption, opportunities for conversations with their adult children, and the pleasures of grandchildren. They are content more with relationship than with acquisition of things, and it is a time when many parents speak of the pleasures rather than the challenges of child-rearing.

Young parents often want to change the old model, the consumption model, to the sustainable model while their children are still young. Of course there are difficulties to do so, and it has to be done together. The sustainable model must begin during the first years of the lives of children in order to let it operate into our lives. At this stage, marriage is basically adding up each day and giving support and strength to your spouse when he or she does not see the light at the end of the tunnel. So many times, when I was really anxious about my work, the organization of a Bahá'í event, or so many things to be done in one day, the simple words of my husband that everything would turn out well or "I will pray for you" would calm me down.

Maury Miloff also shared some of his thinking about the process of raising children. He admitted that it wasn't easy at times:

At certain stages marriage felt like a prison sentence of having to keep your nose to the grindstone, of being on too short a leash. Those were painful times, and I contributed my share of kicking and screaming, blaming, upending, criticizing, and dreaming about exit doors and love in other packages. Actually, I don't know how I got through all those bad times. Fear of really dire consequences, a sense of responsibility, giving it one more time helped. During some of challenging times of raising children, parents need to learn to support one another even more: emotionally, spiritually, and physically. Recognizing the value of perseverance was a valuable lesson and helped us overcome each obstacle with more resources and patience.

I think many couples must go through periods of such intense challenge. Perhaps they have been overcome simply through remembering their love for one another. Maury reminded me:

Really, when the chips were completely down and all reserves seemed exhausted, I would look into the face of my partner and see the burning beauty and fidelity, the memories there of all the most important things in life that we shared and gave each other. I saw, under her sometimes shocked and tired life-worn surface the inexhaustible depths of her purity, love, and inner mystery, and with that came the turning point of enough hope and enough reason to believe that we could, if we just got past the stupid stuff, swim together again in those ancient, beautiful, and heady waters.

Maury appears to have gained more and more appreciation for his wife as they have needed to deal with the challenges of parenthood together. Their children have provided the common bond and glue for their growing love for one another. His comment takes me back to the idea from the introduction, the notion that 'Abdu'l-Bahá, in laying the foundation stone of the temple, said that the temple was built. This is the same ideal offered by Bahá'u'lláh, and the "fortress for well-being" analogy of marriage means that we see the "end in the beginning." This fortress protects both ourselves and the person we have learned to love, have married, and with whom we have shared so much. The fortress symbolizes the promise that the relationship will not end in this lifetime and that it is a gift of spiritual perspective.

My mother often said that she thought that one of the reasons people have children is to learn the spiritual qualities of selflessness, compassion, and hopefulness. Within the marriage, as couples work together in all their endeavors, but perhaps especially as they raise children together, there are many opportunities for them to learn to care about others before themselves, to develop patience, sympathy, empathy, and a profound sense of trust that the future will be full of love. Children are often the cement for love between couples, despite all the challenges that raising them can provide. Children provide a greater opportunity for couples to find unity of purpose and spiritual gratitude.

The Upbringing of the Parents

The upbringing of parents is also important in determining how they will raise their own children. The childhood experiences of parents can either be positive, negative, or more often a combination of both. Peter Brady shared the importance, to him, of his own upbringing in committing himself to his marriage:

I was born in New York City and raised in upstate New York. Both my parents were Catholic, my father nominally because he also investigated the occult. My mother was strongly religious yet progressive in her views about some of the difficulties posed by strict Catholicism. She obeyed the Church to the best of her ability, accepting her situation when she discovered an annulment was not possible. In the sixties she favored the ecumenical movement and encouraged some of her nieces and nephews to also participate. Her religion was the foundation of her life, yet she did not force me to accept it. One of her pieces of advice was the famous line commonly attributed to Voltaire: "I disapprove with what you say, but I will defend to the death your right to say it."*

My parents separated when I was four. This was shortly after World War II, a time when marriages did not display difficulties. When a marriage failed, it was the wife's fault because she could not keep her man. This was a silly notion at the least and downright impossible at the worst. I was raised by my mother, who was a single parent. This is a common occurrence today, but in the 1940s, '50s, and '60s, this was unheard of and shameful. Since my parents often argued by long distance—phone calls or letters—I seldom saw my father, who died when I was forty-seven. It would not be an exaggeration to say that, between age four when they separated and the time of his death, he spent a total of six months with us. As a role model, his example was more negative—i.e., what a husband and father should not be. To ensure our children did not experience this, I often did what I thought was the opposite of what my father would have done or did.

Peter's experience was quite different from that of many of the couples' stories, and it relates to an important part of family life: evaluating the family of your birth and deciding how to apply what you know to your developing family as children are born.

The Nablos felt that life also took on a focus where the children came first. They had six children, one of whom was

---

* The source for this famous quotation is actually Evelyn Beatrice Hall, in *The Friends of Voltaire*, published in 1906. See http://www-users.cs.york.ac.uk/~susan/cyc/l/liberty.htm.

stillborn, but they also became adoptive parents to one child, keeping the total number of children at six.

Ron said,

We have often noted that our first arguments, or, at least, significant differences of opinions came with the patter of little feet. When I wanted to correct a child's misdemeanor, I tended to shout at them. I have no idea where I learned to do that, as I do not recall my parents shouting at us when we were children. I also recognized that Edna's methods, including diverting the child's attention elsewhere, particularly to something positive, was much better, but that did not necessarily change my behavior. On the other hand, we both invented lots of ways of dealing with family problems, some of which worked and some of which did not. The essence of the matter is probably that we both gave a lot of attention to family matters, Edna about 100% of the time, and I 100% of the time when I was home.

Edna added,

When Ron and I married, in the '50s, nearly every magazine you picked up had some article about the "adjustments" that marriage would require. So, we were prepared for them, but the early months of our marriage were filled with so many confirmations that we had made the right decision that the idea of "adjustments" seemed ludicrous. We loved living together and had no trouble at all. This idyllic state continued until, nineteen months later, we had our first child. We then discovered that we were at opposite ends of the pole in terms of how children should be cared for and raised. We both felt very strongly about our own views, and our consultations did not yield any solutions. But this didn't stop us from having two more children rather quickly, and later, three more yet, making six in all. This is how we resolved our differences—it wasn't easy, but in retrospect we think it worked pretty well.

I was curious about how they had "resolved" their differences. Edna commented,

We started with the recognition that being united is more important than being "right," and so, in relation to the children, we would support each other's decisions. Sometimes it took everything we had (each of us) to support a decision that the other had made, but we swallowed our own feelings and did it pretty well, I think, and the result was that we had well-behaved children who did not run from one to the other parent to get support for their own desires. And an interesting thing happened. As the years went by, Ron found that he was developing more sympathy for my approach, and I found that I was developing more sympathy for his. Meanwhile, our marriage and our family were intact.

Keeping a United Front

What seems clear about the approach of these couples is that they did not enter into their marriages with all their ideas worked out, but they were willing to communicate along the way and to recognize one another's abilities to develop a united way of dealing with children—and other elements of their joint lives—together. The lives of their children became, in some respects, so intricately connected with their own lives that the Nablos don't even think about independent goals. This is a theme explored, from a different perspective, by Margaret Bremner, who said,

I have no idea what our relationship would be like without children! We certainly need more living space and stuff, the house is definitely louder, and there are a lot of interesting activities going on. It's easier to meet the neighbors when you have children. We both felt that it was very important for young children to be at home with mom (or at least a parent) and not farmed out to "caregivers." In the long run, I think this affected our family income because I lost out on a decade of workplace experience, seniority, training, whatever. But I think it was good for our children.

Rick and Nahid Gordon also made observations about the challenges raising children can bring, as a constant process of negotiation, to marriage. Rick stated,

Raising children created the greatest challenges in the relationship because of the sense of importance that this held and the widely varying experience and priorities that we brought from our eastern and western cultures. Adherence to or rejection of family patterns was a very significant factor in our disagreements. My awareness of my lack of competence in raising children grew steadily year-by-year as I sought out presentations and literature on the subject. Pre-children training in this area could have had a dramatically positive impact on the results of our efforts. The old adage "If I had only known then what I know now" applied far more to child-raising than any other aspect of married life.

Nahid also noted, "Sometimes the children's comments or actions bring me to the realization of what kind of mistake I have made and how not to repeat it in my relationship."

Peter Brady noted both sides of the equation regarding his children:

Our children have been a source of joy, concern, frustration, irritation, hope, pleasure, and surprise. I say *surprise* because we found that they retained and applied many of the values we tried to teach them. So often when they were teenagers, they seemed to ignore what we tried to tell them; however, they did not and still do not smoke, drink, or take drugs. We are proud that they held on to these values in spite of the pressures of their peers.

I want our children to succeed beyond what I have achieved and sometimes feel frustrated when they repeat the mistakes I made. They have the best of both our families, and we encourage them to find these qualities and use them rather than search out and adopt the character flaws of their parents, uncles, and aunts.

Training Children for Success in Life

The success of their children's lives is, unsurprisingly, an integral part of the thinking of families. Success seems to come as a part of service and its spiritual connection, not because it is the goal. Gord and Cheryl Epp had a lot to say about the effect that children had had on their marital life.

Cheryl said, "We see ourselves as part of a family, and we have always put family first over career choices." For example, she noted, "Gord would love to do art and I would like him to be able to, but it just isn't going to happen much right now. I'd like to write songs and poetry more."

She connected looking after their son, Angus, with their increasing understanding of the importance of family life:

> The ultimate form of service to God is looking after your child when he or she is past being a child. Angus is our son, but he's also a companion. He tells me when it's time to say a prayer and is a form of guidance in our life. The love he gives us and the love we have for him is worth it, and if that's all we do in life, that's enough. You can only see it as a gift and an opportunity, even with all the loss and the grief. Our goal is for his life to be the best it can be, regardless of how long it may be. The benefit of living with loss is learning to live in the moment. Angus's philosophy is "something good has to happen every day." [She laughed.] Even if it means going to Starbucks every day.

Gord concurred. "I expected to have children. It was not a surprise, and I looked forward to it, so having kids was kind

of a fulfillment of myself that left an impression in the world."
He laughed and added,

> Children are not at all what you expect! You're not always faced with the problems you might anticipate. You imagine being surrounded by kids when you're older and having a support system to help them to raise families. We have a certain amount of that with our eldest son. But having kids turned us inside out.
>
> We are doing things differently than I would have thought. I can't even imagine not having kids. Sure, I can imagine myself more involved with my career or helping our faith more, but it would have been a lot more oriented toward my directions and choices rather than serving the needs of others.
>
> I've learned a lot about living for others and about sacrifice by having kids. Having kids opened me up to recognizing the innate value of each individual in the world and serving them—no matter who they are. You don't have to value people for what they've achieved and for who they're going to be. Instead, you love them for the sake of God, and you learn about love with your own kids. Having kids makes you want to do something for people and not to expect something back.
>
> It's not that your creative needs aren't important, it's just that it's the right thing to do, and if you love them, it has a powerful effect on yourself and them. It's all fulfilling, with no need to look for a reward. You just do it, and it's a special opportunity to be close to someone in the world.

Cultural Challenges to Raising Children

Parviz and Gillian Mottahed agreed with Gord and Cheryl and went on to discuss the challenges posed by raising children in a culture different from our own. Parviz said,

Any marriage is the union of two people, both spiritually and emotionally. In mixed marriage, compatibility involves not so much personal differences, but cultural ones, like being strict or relaxed about etiquette. England is permissive, and I couldn't reconcile with the culture even though I was submerged in it for some time. There was a tremendous percentage of things I could not accept. And there comes a time when the problems are accentuated by cultural differences. Where are you going to go from here? You are becoming two-in-one, but cultural differences threaten to push you apart.

Gillian explained, "This also applies to the time when children leave to pursue their own lives. Couples who don't have a family can go along on a pretty even course, but when you have a family, you have to deal with the empty nest syndrome. I was traumatized when our children left home because I was on my own much more than before. Parviz and I talked about this a lot, and dealing with our children's departure is what we're working on together."

Parviz said, "When one grows older, one realizes the role a person plays in one's life. Over the years I have realized [he laughed]—and I hope I'm not being soppy—she is my soul mate. When she was sick two years ago, I was literally pulsating with fear. I had difficulty seeing life without Gill. The main part of my life for her, for our family, and it would have been gone."

He laughed again and said, "I have four 'f' words of life. One, *faith*. Two, *family*. Three, *friends*. Four, *fun*. It's my recipe for life. If I have these, my life is complete. My friends are hers, and hers are mine. There is an intermeshing in our lives."

While raising their children, the Mottaheds both had challenges with health issues; at one point, Parviz had a stroke, and at another time Gillian was also seriously ill. They talked about how that experience had changed them.

Gillian said, "My priorities have changed overnight and I know Parviz's did."

I asked, "How?"

Gillian: "I don't have patience for trivialities. I've let go of many material things, and my tolerance is low for materialism, especially if I feel material objects are being valued out of context. I've cut certain things out of my life, and I'm just grateful to be here."

Parviz added, "We take a lot for granted in life. When health was an issue—when Gill was sick—I thought, oh, I could have lost it all. Once when she was sick in our younger years, I put the children to bed, and I went to our bedroom and thought, what do I need out of life? And I cried. The only thing I need is her health. I need her to be near me."

He added that he had been present for the birth of their grandchildren—having missed the birth of their children—and that he had learned what's most important: "I want to spend more time with Gill!"

6

FINANCIAL AND CULTURAL ISSUES

When such difference of opinion and belief occurs
between husband and wife it is very unfortunate for
undoubtedly it detracts from that spiritual bond
which is the stronghold of the family bond, especially
in times of difficulty. The way, however, that it
could be remedied is not by acting in such wise as to
alienate the other party. One of the objects of the Cause
is actually to bring about a closer bond in the homes.
In all such cases, therefore, the Master* used
to advise obedience to the wishes of
the other party and prayer. . . .
Once that harmony is secured then you will
be able to serve unhampered.

Written on behalf of Shoghi Effendi

In a marriage, it is not always possible to agree. Financial concerns were one area in which several people noted an ongoing need for consultation, and some of these discussions were impacted by the additional challenges of coming from cultures that had different approaches to money. In some cultures, all of the decision-making was made by the husband, and adapting to a more egalitarian approach was a challenge. Other cultures assumed that both the husband and wife should have independence in financial areas, while others consulted about every financial decision, no matter how minute, regardless of the size of the income, or who made the money. I asked the couples I interviewed about how they handled these topics in marriage and how they

---

* 'Abdu'l-Bahá.

maintained harmony when talking about them. Consultation, it seemed, was again a key element in the process of finding agreement about finances and cultural concerns. Consulting about money, like any other area of difference, simply takes on a somewhat more "creative" tone when each partner emphasizes his or her own priorities.

I think there is a culture about money. So many assumptions come from the way we see money handled and the expectation that the way money is dealt with in the home family is the "correct" way of doing things. I asked Ron and Edna Nablo to comment on the financial areas of married life. Their family was "traditional" in having a father who worked outside the home and a mother who worked at home taking care of six children born from 1956 to 1970. Ron was the sole wage earner for most of the marriage. Money was often tight. For the first forty years of their marriage, Ron and Edna had a joint bank account. Who made the money was not an issue for them; what was done with it, however, required considerable consultation since each person's priorities were different. As Edna explained, "Things change. We now have separate accounts for particular interests, in retirement, which works better for us. We still have a joint account, but with our own accounts, we also have some autonomy."

She laughingly noted that this was in theory: really, even after over fifty years of marriage, she said that she and Ron had not yet arrived at a truly satisfactory resolution to their differences in perception about financial matters. Despite this, she agreed when I observed that having an area where one is not able to find resolution does not constitute sufficient reason to give up on a marriage. Learning to consult was key.

Importance of Consultation and Good Communication

Consultation and good communication were probably the two single most important themes that couples noted as essential to understanding how to work together financially. When Don and Diana Dainty met, they were both studying religion and going to different religious meetings. This association led to their declarations of faith in Bahá'u'lláh during February of 1954. The following year they worked together on the Bahá'í Student Group at the University of Toronto. They subsequently discovered they had a mutual interest in tennis, which led to a date to play in the indoor court of the old Collegiate in Forest Hill, Ontario, then North Toronto. Long walks ensued, with much sharing of family history.

I asked them, "Did you fall in love?"

"Oh yes," Don exclaimed instantly, and Diana nodded agreement.

I asked them to describe what falling in love was like for them. They said they had "good communication" and worked well together.

Diana noted, "Values you learn from your parents will come out in your mindset." She then added several points, including the thought that gradually one must reevaluate the lessons and teachings learned from parents. For example, she said, a mother and father's guidance regarding hardship and difficulty can sometimes need modification in new circumstances. Diana and Don had found the Bahá'í writings very helpful in this respect, as they encourage generosity, detachment, and trust in God. This guidance can replace worry

and angst, while prayer and consultation can lead to mutually agreed upon solutions. Diana mentioned in this context
that one of her favorite passages from 'Abdu'l-Bahá was:
"Mutual helpfulness and cooperation are the two necessary
principles underlying human welfare."[1]

When speaking of money, Don noted, "We've been fortunate."

Diana added, "He's always had gainful employment, and
he is a generous man who has never complained about
money."

The couple explained their system. "Di does homework
on big expenditures, and we don't buy big items without
consulting."

Having a Common Vision

Consultation and good communication are themes that
many couples saw as essential to understanding how to work
together financially. Ovidio Gomez expressed it this way:
"Where I notice a difference, in a lot of my friends and family, is the trouble they have in handling money. We haven't
had a lot of income, but we have a common vision of what
we want in life, and I think that helps us. We don't fight
about money."

His wife Coral added, "There are little differences in
money—like I spend a little on toys."

Ovidio interjected, "But I don't get mad. A lot of the fights
I see are about money—young people should talk about it."

Coral: "And we never had separate agendas involving
money. It didn't matter who made it. Maybe it's because we

don't have a lot of extra money floating around. Any extra we did have went into our house."

June Barrow noted the tensions that can arise when asked about money.

I asked, "Is money a pressure?"

They answered, "Yes, but it's slight because we are always somehow 'rescued' by God, or relatives, or something. There have been many times when we were very poor and in debt, and we never seemed to have things such as savings, retirement, or anything like that. Yet we've always had what we needed at any given time, so we don't put a high priority on worrying about it. Reg is more detached than I am about this one, as I hate being in debt and would like to get out of it, but probably it's precisely because I'm so hung up on that issue that it doesn't happen."

Margaret Bremner expressed a similar idea in response to the same question. When asked if money was a pressure, she said:

> Oh, you betcha. We've only had a total of maybe four years when the family had a relatively decent income. Mostly our fingernails are always pretty worn down scraping by and trying to hang on. It's very difficult when you want the children to be able to do something, or get repairs made, or buy for quality, or whatever, and you just can't. We have owned a clothes dryer for four of our twenty-six years of marriage. Thank God for Medicare. Early in our marriage we were discussing difficulties people might have to deal with (health, marital, financial, problem children, etc.) and commented that if we had to have one, we'd probably choose financial. We should have kept our mouths shut!

Stuart North also explained that money can be an issue, especially as so much of the Norths' marriage has been given to serving others:

> We still have two mortgages to pay off, which will take several more years. We have been supporting one of our daughters and her two very young children while her husband took some specialized job training. Other family members require quite specialized diets because of food allergies. We do not have a retirement nest egg and will continue to work for as long as we are able. We are fortunate to have a successful business since finding full-time work when you are in the fifty-five through sixty-five years age bracket is quite challenging. We are able to maintain a good income, provided we both work, but we quickly start digging into our savings if the income of either of us is reduced or nonexistent for a period of time.

Flexibility

Financial difficulties appear to require a considerable flexibility within marriage. Peter and Muguette Brady talked frankly about the challenges a lack of money has provided. Peter said,

> Money is a source of many discussions, some arguments, and many of our prayers. We both come from blue-collar backgrounds where money or lack of it often presented problems. Perhaps it is the one area where I have the least faith.

Growing up very poor remains a major influence in much of my thinking. From experience, I know that God provides, and He has done so on many occasions, but not every time and not in the massive amounts. We live simply and relatively comfortably. No doubt we live better than our parents did, but we don't live better than many of our friends.

His wife Muguette noted, "Money has been a pressure sometimes, and it continues to be one for us. It's an area where I have to work all the time to resist my impulses. But I know I have made some progress in this area."

Learning to Budget

Parviz and Gillian Mottahed had an appreciation for the times when they had learned to budget together. Like many of the other couples, Gillian and Parviz Mottahed are eloquent on the subject of the importance of their children in their lives, although Gillian noted that the sixteen-month period that they had before the arrival of their first child, Dara, was blissful, carefree, and "a real adventure." The classic "honeymoon" phase almost always yields to a different reality with the arrival of children, and the Mottaheds were no exception. Parviz was still a student, and Gillian was at home with Dara. They reminisced about this stage of their lives fondly, in part because in encountering hardships together, it forged a greater bond between them.

Gillian noted, "I'm glad we had that time. By this time Parviz was back in the university taking a second degree, and naturally the money was tight because he was a student. The sense of togetherness and lack of luxuries of life helped us. Though we worked hard and life was a struggle, we lived very happily, eating well and traveling to see family and friends. We were very happy, and our pleasures were very simple."

Parviz interjected, "We are both very social: we like dancing, the cinema, giving dinner parties, and so on."

Gill picked up, in the same breath, "We somehow managed, even though our means were limited."

Parviz said, "We thrive on friends and family, and I always have people coming and going. This has been like this as far back as I remember."

Gillian added, "It was magical for me, and we really just loved each other's company."

Parviz continued, "You have to go back into yourself, your childhood, reflect, get clearer. I didn't sacrifice principle." He laughed and gives an example. "Our daughter, Parisa, married the first man in her life. I never used the word *boyfriend*, I don't like the word boyfriend. It would be a major compromise for me to use the word boyfriend; I think it's strange that even seventy-year-old friends will say they had a visit from their boyfriend. I always said, 'friend of the family.' The children always laughed, but it went deeper than language—the whole notion of boyfriend and girlfriend. . . ."

I asked if there had been more challenges during the children's adolescence.

Gillian said, "Yes—isn't this the same with any growing youth? One has to set limits and boundaries."

Parviz added another example: "With Dara, I said, I will pay for your education. But if I do this, I expect you to work." He added, "It was sometimes a challenge, with two children in university. Their job was to go through the courses and pass. They were not expected to work and pay their way, as is the common practice in the West. My father paid for my education at university until such time as I could see myself through financially. That was the time that he stopped, at my request. With our family, needless to say, the finances were tight. Keeping the family going and paying for two youths in university took a chunk out of our expenses."

Much later, they both shared, "We wanted to be around the children, with or without money. As retired persons we don't need too much to live on. Our lives are dedicated to our children and grandchildren. It's for them that we're in Ottawa, suffering through the cold winter. It's for the kids."

I asked them if they ever "fought" or argued.

Gillian laughed, "Oh yeah. But not about money! I can't imagine not arguing."

But Parviz added, "Mostly it's that ten percent of trespassing on cultural demarcation lines . . ."

Gillian said, "That touches a nerve. Now that Parviz is at home, naturally there are more occasions to transgress the 'line on the sand.' Retirement is hard. It was imposed on us overnight because of the health issue, so the biggest adjustments have been in the last six years."

Parviz said, "We now have 100% exposure all day long, which naturally results in more arguments. So you try and learn from it, life goes on." Parviz also explained,

I abhor the relationship when the couple refer to "things" as "my this," "my that." When you become a couple, when one enters the sacred institution of marriage, "my this" and "my that" becomes "our." When we were in Abadan, Iran, we had other friends in similar situations as ourselves, with intercultural marriages, small children, and so on. The wives chose to work outside the home, and they left the children at home with a local untrained nanny, who had no idea about raising children and had a total lack of familiarity with either culture. We consulted about this, and we came to the conclusion that it was in the best interests of Dara, and later Parisa, that Gillian stay at home. We could do without the financial benefit, as the pay for an expatriate employee was very lucrative. We don't like it when marriage becomes a commercial entity instead of becoming the home of love. Hardship has its own advantages, as we said before.

Rick and Nahid Gordon had some observations about culture and financial affairs. Nahid noted, of her Persian background, "My upbringing was somewhat protective, and my expectation of a man as a husband was that he should take care of, protect, support, and understand me. This was a very unrealistic picture that didn't help me with my relationship. I think and feel very much differently than I did many years ago in Iran. I am more expressive now compared to a long time ago."

Rick added,

We consult seriously and effectively about all major purchases, resulting in negligible resentment later. We have faced more challenges when making decisions regarding child rearing, where it was far more difficult to be certain which solution would be best and to achieve the goal once the decision was made.

A significant decision had an important positive impact on our financial affairs. We decided to automatically transfer a fixed amount of funds from my regular income to each spouse's personal account as "crazy" money. Also, any of my overtime earnings went to my personal account, and any of Nahid's earnings went to her personal account. Each spouse had the complete independence to decide how to spend his or her money. We decided how to spend all remaining common funds by consulting until we reached a united position. This strategy created unity regarding all major financial decisions. It also allowed each person the freedom to pursue private goals without feeling guilty for spending too much on items of no interest to the spouse. We feel that learning financial responsibility can be assisted by consulting to create a budget and then allowing each person the freedom to spend funds as he or she wishes within those limits. I do not know if these ideas will be of any help to you, but they have been of considerable help to us.

Rick also had some general observations about the impact of their different cultures on their marriage. He said,

I have often found men to be more task-oriented and direct in communication than women. Their thinking tends to be less tightly focused and more aware of everything happening around them. Their ability to communicate with each other at times seems to me to be like Vulcan "mind-melding." Although Persian tradition influences my wife far less than many other people from that country, my English / Scottish background was sufficiently different from hers to result in some serious challenges, especially regarding child-raising. I have observed similar differences in other mixed marriages, so young couples would do well to anticipate a perilous passage through this marital "Strait of Magellan" if they are not sufficiently prepared for marriage.

Culture has a varying degree of impact, it seems, on marriages, but all the couples in cross-cultural marriages remarked on the importance of time, change, and patience with each other.

Travel During Marriage

June Barrow, who has led a fulfilling life both as a mother and as a professional teacher and school principal, noted that she and her husband had experienced many tests while pioneering in Cameroon. What had helped them through the hardships had been their faith in God. She said, "In marriage, there may be many things that you might view as 'tests' but that have helped you and your partner build a solid foundation. For example, there was a time in the early days of Cameroon's thirteen years when we had no jobs, no house, no car, no furniture, and no money, but the NSA [the national governing body of the Bahá'ís in Cameroon] asked us to stay in the country. We simply obeyed, and we jointly decided that if we had faith, things would somehow work out."

There is a quote attributed to 'Abdu'l-Bahá, and it reads, "As you have faith, so shall your powers and blessings be."[2] This quote is well known to most Bahá'ís, and seems to have been an underpinning for Reggie and June's early time in Cameroon. In any case, their prayers seem to have been answered affirmatively, as June narrated:

Before too long, we ended up with all those things in one way or another—Reg started his own business (with great difficulty in a French West African environment), and I was offered a job running a school through the referral of a friend. Then, quite "out of the blue," the NSA asked us to keep their "mobile institute" vehicle for awhile, and we were literally given a beautiful home with a pool by a friend who asked us to watch it. We didn't have to pay any rent until we had money, and a carpenter we knew built us several pieces of beautiful furniture. He said he trusted us and that we could pay him when we had money (we had previously given him pictures of "what we might like someday when we had the money" but never expected him to go ahead and make it then!). At this time, the boys got free tuition at the school that offered me the job, and I could go on and on with all the bounties that came to us as a result of just having faith and praying to God.

We didn't realize what we'd been through until years later when a friend said, "I can't believe how you two went through all those tests," and we said, "We did?"

Anyway, reflecting back on that and many other similar times has given us a tangible example of how a family can grow through these kinds of "tests"—just the realization that there is nothing more important than trying to serve and being detached, and also just the great bounties and blessings that seem to come from having faith in God.

Gender Roles

Some couples noted that they had been raised with different ideas about the roles of men and women in family finances. Stuart North noted the importance of the way he had been raised to his attitudes about finances:

I grew up in the U.K. during the '50s and '60s. My father was a well-educated engineer and the sole income earner. My mother stayed at home and was a traditional housewife. My perception of marriage was that I would work to bring in the family income and that my wife would raise the children and take care of the house, meals, and so on. Our married life was like this for six years after we started having children, but after living overseas, my wife and I both worked full time. Since returning to Canada, my role in the running of the house has increased, and my portion of the family income has decreased. This has been a difficult adjustment for me. My wife is happy she is making a good income since she doesn't feel constrained in the way it is spent.

These attitudes to finances seem different to current North American values systems, where people put off marriage for years in order to become financially stable before they marry and have children. A common theme appears to be that marriages can develop new strengths in having to overcome financial difficulties. The need for communication was repeated by every couple as a basic need of the marriage. Bruce Filson, Margaret Bremner's husband, commented further, "Consultation is key. We consult *all* the time, night and day."

He commented, regarding money, "Money has *always* been our bugbear. We have lived for over twenty-five years well under the so-called poverty line. Both of us were raised in middle, even upper middle-class, lifestyles, so it's never been easy to get used to. But when we married we both knew we wanted to pursue our personal art (visual art and literature), and we knew that doing so probably meant financial sacrifice, so we've had a kind of tacit contract."

Margaret commented, "We need to know that our partner has our best interests at heart. We need to be supported in our endeavors and supportive of our partner in his or hers."

Bill and Phoebe Anne Lemmon also shared their approach to finances: "Considering his farm background, Bill displays remarkable flexibility in helping with housework. The kitchen is still largely Phoebe Anne's domain. Money is not an issue. Cash in the box is spent as required by either and replenished as needed. Neither of us is extravagant. Phoebe Anne has some bank accounts and a credit card in her name, which gives her a sense of security and independence."

Communication and consultation seem to be very important for couples dealing with finances. Ron Nablo tells the
story of how financial perspectives were a recurrent theme of
discovery for him and for his wife. He said,

> Edna and I discovered later in life that we have very differ-
> ent ways of approaching the handling of money. Edna grew
> up in a very poor family in east end Toronto. Her father was
> on welfare during the depression years and was unemployed
> other years, whereas my father, as an electrical engineer, was
> employed through the depression, and he reached the peak
> of his profession with Ontario Hydro during the war years.
> He was able to pay cash for the fourth Dodge car that came
> into Toronto after the war. I was not aware if my parents had
> debts or not, but I know we did, and I did not know how
> much Edna hated debt until much later in life.
>
> We did not discover until our early forties that we en-
> joyed certain ways of spending money together, such as at
> auctions. We went to auctions in Saskatchewan and had a
> ball. Edna bought many of the family groceries in bulk
> there, and I bought animals for the farm. Much later, when
> we had returned to Canada from Belize for financial rea-
> sons, Edna initiated a small secondhand business. . . . In
> the process of helping with the business, my inclination
> to want things to be bigger and faster led to our renting a
> large two-floor building downtown and getting seriously
> into furniture, rather than just clothing and jewelry. It
> worked, and we worked together attending auctions and
> garage sales to purchase our secondhand goods. I had a
> tendency to buy larger and larger items, while Edna was

always more cautious. But our combination worked very well on the whole.

Edna recalled her view of marriage and money during the time she and Ron were thinking of marrying:

What did seem important to me, since the likelihood was that for several years I would be a stay-at-home mom, was that I choose someone who, in addition to being physically attractive to me, was likely to be a good father and would be absolutely faithful. Secondly, because I have an independent streak, I wanted someone who would never use money as a weapon during the years when I was economically dependent. I think I chose well. Ron was and is a good father, he has never been unfaithful, and he has never used money as a weapon. Sometimes he hasn't used it too wisely, but he's never used it as a weapon.

Ron noted that their attitude to money led to their children having a certain degree of flexibility: "Our teenage children at this stage experienced a rather unstable house. However, as we began to advertise the sale of our household furniture, we discovered to our amazement that we were selling more from the house than we were from the store, so we began to backfill the house from the store. The kids would leave the house in the morning, having sat at one kitchen suite, and come home to eat supper on another, or sit on a new living room suite!"

There was, however, an upside to this seeming chaos: "We always kept the best things in the house for our own use, so we ended up with a very well furnished house. . . . Again, Edna and I would never have predicted that we would both have enjoyed the process so much. She was more cautious, and I would take much greater risks. In discussing the mutual pleasure now, we agree that it was getting a great bargain that gave us the most satisfaction."

Ron, who holds a master's degree in sociology, had worked for many years of their marriage with the federal government of Canada in senior management positions. However, he was quite happy to diversify his interests and assist his wife in developing her entrepreneurial talents—first in the secondhand business and later in Belize, where they started a bakery that is still in operation and that has financially assisted extended family members as well.

Financial Independence

Like the Nablos, Bob LeBlanc and his wife Louise had to work out a satisfactory way of dealing with financial affairs. They noted that they were currently in a period of transition. In the Yukon, both had held good jobs, but Bob had managed the joint bank account. Louise didn't like that because she felt "answerable" to him for her expenditures. So they agreed to create an account for Louise so that she could do "whatever" she wanted with that money. Louise said, "I needed that independence."

Now, they are in different circumstances, as they have moved, and Bob is still in transition with work. Louise laughed and said that now "I spend and face the consequences."

Bob said, "You just buy what **you want** anyway."

But he noted also that in this time of change, "She's so patient. When we had a lot, we just spent more; now, we just spend less."

Louise added, "We're in sacrificial times."

Neither was too worried about the need for sacrifice.

Cultural Differences

Parviz and Gillian Mottahed also shared views about the complex interweaving of family needs, cultural differences, and financial affairs. When Dara Mottahed was born, Parviz said that it was both a happy time and a sad one. He was not present for his son's birth, and he did not actually meet Dara until he was two months old. He had been sent to Iran on business, and Gillian stayed with her mother for the two months before the birth. Gillian did not travel to Iran to join Parviz until Dara was safely old enough to travel. Parviz noted, "I received a telegram that read, 'you are a proud father.'" He noted that this was in a time before telephone and Internet communication offered speedy connection. He added, almost as an afterthought, "Dara was almost nine pounds. My first feeling of fatherhood, though—the feeling that we were two who had become three—came later."

He interjected a perspective of culture: "In my culture, we don't watch childbirth, but the father is always there to greet his new son or daughter. In my case, I wasn't there to hold the child, so I made up for it by making sure I was there to hold all my grandchildren. But back to when Dara was born—it was only when Gillian arrived in Abadan two months later and I got to see my baby for myself that I realized our lives now had new responsibilities. Everything had changed." He spoke of his feelings for Gillian's courage of coming into his culture: "Especially with a Western bride coming to an Eastern culture, even though the town we lived in was Westernized, her experiencing it—my wife, my bride, mother of my child, coming to a place where everything was strange—it really took courage. It made me realize how much I loved her."

He paused.

Gillian said,

Dara was born when I was twenty-two. I went to live with Mom; I had to transfer hospitals: the two months waiting for the baby were very hard, emotionally, for me, but I also had to manage without Parviz. This was not an easy task, but once Dara arrived, life was busy getting ready for the journey to join Parviz in a country I knew little about. At the same time the thought of leaving my mother, who loved Dara, was rather daunting. It must have been traumatic for her, as no one knew much about Iran, but I never once wavered about joining Parviz. It was one of the most difficult times of my life, to see my mom and my sister waving at Heathrow, weeping. They didn't know when they would see me again. And I was young for my age, but conflicting emotions couldn't stop me.

Parviz noted, "We're talking the '60s, when there was limited communication. It was not like now, where if someone trips in Baghdad we know it instantly, or where we talk about Botswana or a South Pacific island and even vacation there. All the world knew about Iran were Persian carpets and Persian cats; that was it. Iran was a mystical place, a mystery for Gillian's family."

Parviz and Gillian's daughter Parisa was born in Iran. Parviz laughed, somewhat ruefully, "I missed that one too because Gillian's mom was arriving in Abadan! I took her home from the airport and went to see Gillian, but they said at the hospital that I had time to go home, put Dara to bed and take care of Gillian's mother. I arrived back at 10:45, and Parisa had been born ten minutes earlier and moved to the nursery. I had to wait until the next day to hold her in my arms."

Their third child, Fiona, was born in the north of England, some three years after they got back from Iran. Parviz was continuing his higher education. This was another move and another way of doing things for Dara and Parisa.

They spoke a great deal about culture, noting that Parviz told the children, "You have parents who are the products of two different cultures, East and West." One area where this was true was in resolving disagreements.

Gillian shared that the arrival of their first child was also the "first major cause of disagreement as far as the upbringing of the child is concerned."

Parviz added, "Naturally, when the family lived in Iran— that is, during the first three years of Dara's life—because of the fact that we were surrounded by the Iranian culture, it was natural for the influence of the Iranian culture to be predominant in our lives. When we came back to the U.K., by virtue of the geography and predominance of Western culture, then naturally there had to be a role reversal."

Gillian explained, "I didn't have problems with money or possessions, but Parviz was brought up in an environment where parents were the sole 'directors.' Parviz emulated the way he knew best, and as I had no real male influence in my life, it was difficult to understand his approach. I thought he was harsh in his approach, and I was, like many mothers, the buffer."

Parviz interjected, "She still is."

Bill and Phoebe Anne Lemmon, in telling their story, also referred to the mother as "the buffer." Theirs is also a marriage with interesting challenges; here is their story, as they wrote it to me:

We married in 1972, a second marriage for both of us. Phoebe Anne was a widow, and Bill's first marriage had ended in divorce. Rather than a stars-in-the-eyes, butter-flies-in-the-stomach love, our feelings were of the deeper sort. Our admiration and respect for one another preceded our romantic love for one another.

When we married, Phoebe Anne's children were seven, eleven, and twelve years old, and Bill's children, who were ages ten and thirteen, were living with his first wife in England. Bill moved in with Phoebe Anne and her three children, and the early years of our marriage were very difficult because of the multiple adjustments to be made. Different personalities, different parenting styles, the inevitable adolescence of our children—all contributed to tension in the household. Then we moved to Western

Quebec with Bill in a new, demanding job, and this added to the adjustments. Phoebe Anne served as a kind of buffer between Bill and the children. All relationships improved after the children were on their own.

The Lemmons also noted a very practical view of marriage, and they again emphasized spiritual factors over romance: "The primary unifying factor in our marriage has always been faith. We both put our faith first in our lives. Our Bahá'í activities provide our companionship since our other interests are different."

They continued to note the qualities that have united them for over thirty-two years:

> Sexual attraction is certainly a factor in considering marriage, but it is the spiritual qualities that are the cement that holds a marriage together. We have found that consultation and flexibility are invaluable. We've learned that decisions involving both of us should not be made unilaterally by one of us. This is because a unilateral decision is likely to be based on incomplete information. Flexibility is vital to settling differences. When you are on different sides of the fence, you both have to move in order to come together. Granted, it is better in some situations for one to climb over the fence, in which case the other must be patient and supportive during the process.

Bill and Phoebe Anne collaborated to send their observations, and they shared their attitude to different points of view: "When there are differences, we talk them out, although sometimes there is a period of chill air and silence before the talking begins. Our version of 'Don't go to bed on a quarrel' is a morning kiss and a bedtime kiss with 'good-bye' and 'hello' kisses when appropriate. A warm hug is always appreciated. Serious differences are few and far between at this stage of our lives and marriage."

Developing a Culture of Family

Tracy Khajavi observed that the culture of family was important: "Ali, growing up in Iran, had a great example of what a relationship looks like. There were lots of sacrifices made, such as earning money and giving it to the family so everyone could eat. Lots of hardships made his family all very close. For me, being from Canada, I got to see my parents divorce when I was twelve. We were also not well off, but our family is not very close now. We struggle at it."

Tracy had experienced parental divorce at a young age, and like Gillian Mottahed, was attracted to someone from another culture. Overcoming hardship together can provide a special way of increasing the bonds between a husband and wife. Culture can have an impact.

Tracy noted further, "I grew up in Canada, and I'm very used to many different things. I don't even know what my culture is. My husband Ali is very much in love with his culture. I don't see that much difference. Our characters are similar; we seem to like life pretty much the same way."

Pierre Martel also offered a perspective on culture:

I'm not saying anything new by stating that real married life is very different from what I had imagined when I was a youth and single. Kamachee and I have been married for thirty years now (since 1976). She is of Indian origin, born in Malaysia. I am French Canadian. It would be difficult to find two more different cultures. We met in Africa. Kamachee was pioneering in Cameroon, and I was pioneering in Sénégal at the time. I always strongly felt, and still do, that it was through the special intervention of God that we met each other. In other words, there was never a doubt in my mind that we were destined for each other.

This thought picked up on how Gillian Mottahed had expressed herself. That there is a divine purpose to marriage is part of the Bahá'í teachings. One of the Bahá'í prayers reads, "Whatever God hath willed hath been, and that which He hath not willed shall not be."[3] This does not remove free will, but it acknowledges that Bahá'ís believe in a very active, present sense of the divine in their lives.

This belief can help people sustain healthy marriages. Pierre Martel explained, "This has been something very important for me in keeping us together and united. I don't really believe that one has a 'soul mate.' For example, I don't believe that there is only one person on this earth with whom I would have been happy in marriage and that this person is Kamachee. People seem to be using this argument sometimes to justify a divorce. However, I do believe that, if we turn to God, He will place on our path a person that is suitable for us and with whom we can be happy, if we put forth the necessary efforts."

7

THROUGH ADVERSITY TO VICTORY

The true marriage . . . of Bahá'ís is this, that
husband and wife should be united both physically
and spiritually, that they may ever improve the spiritual life
of each other, and may enjoy everlasting unity
throughout all the worlds of God. This is Bahá'í marriage.
—'Abdu'l-Bahá

In the practice of any faith, there are some quotations that become so familiar that they become "favorites." Such a quotation, for me, is one I shared previously, attributed to 'Abdu'l-Baha, the son of Bahá'u'lláh, the Founder of the Bahá'í Faith. 'Abdu'l-Bahá said, "As you have faith, so shall your powers and blessings be."[1]

I like to think of the sustenance of faith as an underpinning for the couples here. Despite the challenges they encountered, to which they speak eloquently, these couples found that persevering in their marriages helped to bring many blessings. They developed a sense of gratitude for the spiritual in their lives, they grew in friendship for each other, shared in the many joys of family life, and are now enjoying the rich bounties of mutual companionship and love within marriages that succeed. To achieve this, they often had to work hard. In this chapter, you will find some astonishing stories of people whose commitment to their marriage endured formidable odds, and not only survived, but survived happily.

The Courage to Grow Together

Of the many couples who shared their stories, perhaps no couple demonstrated more courage than David and Belinda Erickson. At first, when I asked them if they wanted to con-

tribute to the book, Belinda asked, "Can we use a pseud-
onym?" At that stage, I thought they could, so I said yes.
Then they came over for the interview, and as their story
emerged, I asked them how strongly they felt about using
different names. They thought about it, and finally Belinda
exclaimed, "Oh, what the heck. Use our names. If it helps
anyone, it's worth it!" David immediately agreed.

Elopement

David Erickson and Belinda Forsee's story is one that was
beset with challenges, but they shared it openly so that people
could understand that marriage can survive and grow in the
face of what may seem impossible odds. They also attribute
the fact that they are still married, happily, to the spiritual
connection they forged in spite of many external difficulties.
David came from a Jewish family, and Belinda, from a Gen-
tile background. They eloped. I asked them why.

Belinda explained, "Our families were divided, so we said,
'Let's just cut to the chase and present them with a *fait ac-
compli.*'"

David added, "Our families were divided. My parents were
divided because Belinda wasn't Jewish."

Belinda said, "It was more overtly his parents. I know my
parents had objections that were more personal. To be blunt,
my mother noticed the nature of some of David's problems,
and she didn't like him because he reminded her of herself.
She was an alcoholic."

David said, "What about your father?

Belinda noted further, "I can't remember my father ever
saying anything remotely negative about you, but I can remember my mother being more critical. When we decided

to get married, David called a couple of rabbis. One we went to in Hamilton counseled us to be patient." She laughed. "That lasted about two seconds."

David said, "Then we went to a Unitarian minister, who married us."

I asked why they had wanted to marry.

David noted, "We met at university, and Belinda had already been going to the University of Western Ontario before I came on the scene. We were introduced in the cafeteria. I came by and a friend from Toronto."

Belinda interjected, "I had come from Chicago and I could relate to these people, who were a circle of Jewish students from Toronto. They were a little more sophisticated."

David added, "So I was introduced."

Belinda said, "We started hanging out together and eating together. He was this dark-eyed, dark-haired, intense, skinny, cute-looking guy, and the dark eyes got me."

David said, "I wasn't sure what attracted me to Belinda at that time."

Belinda interjected, "Yeah, I'd like to know now."

Laughter.

David continued, "She was very different. She was unlike anyone I'd known before. It was her mind. She was very intellectual, she had a very good mind; we could talk about all kinds of things, no matter what. It was a free-flowing, continual conversation. We could talk about anything whatsoever. So there was already that kind of harmony. It was very, very good that way. And you know, she also didn't dress like many of the other women, either . . . it singled her out more. There was a physical attraction as well . . . but really, I found her interesting as a person, and I felt very much at home with her."

Belinda notes, "I would say the same thing. He was really interested in his courses. He wasn't just there to get a degree."

David emphasized, "But we didn't go out. We didn't have a date for at least a year and a half."

Belinda added, "That was his problem, not mine."

Belinda told David that she was "pissed off" because he really wasn't moving in that direction as much as she would have liked. David was not very sure of himself. So in the fall, they did many things together, went to movies, out to dinner, they went to the London Little Theater.

David offered, "I think that was the year we first slept together."

Belinda laughed, "I could tell you the date."

David noted, "It wasn't long after that we told our parents that we wanted to get married."

Shortly thereafter, after the elopement, they discovered that they were expecting their first child. They hadn't really noticed. Then, as David says, "There was all the trouble, and I never felt accepted by Belinda's mother."

So the families did not accept each other, and Belinda noted that while her parents never accepted him, David's mother did accept her, and as Belinda put it, his mother also "had the guts" to apologize.

First Child

David paused here to reminisce a little about their "honeymoon," which they shared one night in a city hotel. It was a stormy night, which suited their mood. It put a shadow on the occasion, with David asking himself, "What have I done?"

Belinda said, "We were both terrified."

I was curious about how that was resolved.

Belinda: "I don't think we did resolve it, for a long time. The horrible things David's parents had said took root, and David treated me as though they were true."

David: "I seemed to have an unconscious intimation of how difficult it was going to be. I remember telling Belinda that it would not be easy. I was warning her."

Belinda: "I didn't pay attention."

David: "I knew there was something that was going to be bad, but I didn't know what—and it was, it was terrible. Our first year, we rented a flat, and in the course of that time, Pam was born."

Belinda added, "Before that, David was hospitalized for depression. The dynamic of our marriage was very important because he suffered from bipolar depression, but in those days no one knew, and the medication didn't work, and a lot of his depression came out as anger. I took the brunt of it, and I had no idea how to deal with it."

David: "And I was helpless, I didn't know how to deal with it, either. It was a torrent of negative imagery behind everything; all the poisons I had absorbed from my birth family came pouring out in our marriage."

Belinda: "And it was—again—decades before I understood that."

David continues, "I was poisoned by my father's ways of thinking and acting. It was my mother too, in another sense, but my identity was criss-crossed. I wasn't able to identify with my father, which was not good for a boy. I identified with my mother, who was possessive."

Belinda: "Looking back, we realize that the mood disorder interfered with any attempts David made to resolve these things."

David: "I went into marriage without a sense of self. I had no creative identity whatsoever. I had all these negative impulses, acting out my father's rage."

He noted, "I was actually a happy kid, accepting, but the changes had begun."

Belinda: "Your mother always said the changes began when you were five or six, and she didn't understand it."

Separation

I interjected, "This sounds like hell. How did you survive it?"

Belinda: "We didn't. I left. I took Pam and went."

David: "I was so mistrustful . . . I went into rages . . . I was pretty well nonfunctional. I was totally dependent on her. And then her mother got in on the situation."

Belinda said, "I gotta tell you, the months I spent at home with my mother were almost as bad. I almost took off on them. I came close to going back to Chicago. But instead, I went back to school."

David: "And I left and went home to my parents, totally bewildered. I felt like I was a monster, but I knew that I wasn't really that kind of a person, and I didn't want to be that way. So I spent the next few years trying to find out what was going on. I went to three psychiatrists."

Belinda noted, "Fat lot of use they were to you."

David: "I didn't want to be with my parents. I didn't want to stay with them. I would hole up in my bedroom, and they wouldn't see me. I took on new experiences. I tried many things, some of them dangerous. I was trying to find out who I was, find out what kind of person I really was."

I asked how they got back together.

Belinda: "While David was busy finding himself—and he was—those experiences gave him a knowledge of his identity."

She turned to David and said,

You gave yourself the experiences you needed . . . Anyway, I went to school, and at this point I came into contact with the Bahá'í Faith. I had been in contact with Bahá'ís in the '50s, but David didn't know I had a connection with them, and I got back into the Faith during this time.

That's when I started hanging out with Melba Loft, a good Bahá'í friend of mine, who noticed that I was still very angry with David. Four years had passed, and we didn't even have a legal separation. She felt something ought to be done, and she convinced me to go see a lawyer and start the process of getting a divorce.

At the time, Ontario law required proof of infidelity on the part of one spouse in order for the other spouse to initiate divorce proceedings. Belinda's lawyer suggested to David's lawyer that David could come forward and confess to being unfaithful to his wife so that the divorce proceedings could begin. As David had been completely faithful to Belinda throughout their marriage, he naturally refused to accept this arrangement.

Another Chance

Belinda said, "By this time I was thinking that David and I should talk, which was what Melba had had in mind all along."

David said, "And I had a powerful dream in which a wall disappeared, and light was coming in—pouring in—an infusion of light. I knew it was something good. So Belinda and I met and spent hours talking."

Belinda added, "And the upshot of it was that we decided to try again."

Belinda noted, "In the process of this conversation, I told David that I was a Bahá'í."

David's response was very positive. David had been taking a course in politics. This was during the first years of the Kennedy administration, and everybody was hopeful. The professor, who was not a Bahá'í himself, mentioned the Bahá'í Faith in a positive manner, a fact of which David said, "I kind of shelved it in the back of my mind. Now all these years had gone by, after the University of Western Ontario, and we got back together."

Of the meeting with Belinda, David says, "When we met for that time, she told me she was a Bahá'í, and what she told me made sense. So I was very accepting of it, so after we got back together again, a year later, I became a Bahá'í."

Their daughter was five years old. In the ensuing years, two sons were born to them.

David added, "About Melba Loft. Her thinking was not that we should get back together; it was that we should do one thing or another. She wanted to meet me."

Belinda notes, "Melba recognized that underneath all that anger, I actually loved him, which was why I was angry. And her family was a family that believed in marriage and was a family that had also survived marriage. They were great role models."

David: "And she liked me. I was able to talk with Melba, I fit in well with the family, and the Lofts were the pivotal point, so to speak, of why our marriage got back together."

Belinda: "They were Bahá'í role models."

She added, "Before we got married, I remember asking David if he believed in God. And he said yes, and it was really important to me. If he had said no, I think the relationship would not have continued. This, despite the fact that I thought I was a bit of an atheist or an agnostic at the time. But it was important. I think there has always been a spiritual aspect in our relationship, even when we didn't know it."

Tests and the Spiritual Connection

David picked up the theme and said, "The thing about our relationship is that there has always been a common point. I loved her, but I didn't know how to express it. I was no expert on feelings at that time. And when you're not really communicating with your own self in a creative and constructive manner, you don't know how to communicate with others. But I felt that we (Belinda and I) shared something. Still, there were these difficulties, but there was a deeper layer, and it was a spiritual one—although that didn't come out for many years."

Belinda: "It kept us going, but the mood disorder was still there."

David: "The third guy I saw thought I had healed myself, and that was a lot of baloney. But I went to see another psychiatrist, and he was useful."

Belinda: "We had continued to have a lot of conflict but we got marriage counseling, which helped a little, got us through the tough times, and helped us come to grips with what was actually going on."

David noted that he had told Belinda they were going to repeat the process, they were going to repeat the pattern, and they were going to make the same mistakes.

But, David added, "There was a dynamic, a process, that eventually led to our liberation."

Belinda: "We went to see a friend in the hospital, and as she described what was going on with her, David turned to me and said, 'Perhaps I'm a mini-manic.' I took that seriously, so I did some reading, and David went to a new psychiatrist."

David: "The doctor, in 1982, recognized that I was a manic-depressive and put me on lithium. A year later, I started drinking and became an alcoholic."

Belinda explained that David had abstained from alcohol for a long time, but that because the disease picks up where it would have been had the person still been drinking, one drink sent David into "middle-stage alcoholism."

Ironically, Belinda said it was "the best thing that could have happened. You can't cure a disease if you don't know what it is. If someone breaks a leg, you don't put the arm in a sling. After identifying the bipolar depression and the alcoholism, we knew what we were dealing with. And the twelve-step program deals with so many aspects of life—psychological, spiritual, emotional, everything."

The implications for their marriage were significant.

Belinda: "The lithium helped. It was a lot easier to talk to David, and it was easier to get along with our lives."

David: "I was irresponsible because I spent a lot of money."

Belinda: "But you were in the grip of the disorders."

David: "The financial stress was tremendous."

It took seven years of drinking before, in 1990, David went to AA and Belinda went to Al-Anon (a support group for relatives of alcoholics). "It was during the years from 1990 on," said David, "that Belinda and I got a handle on ourselves, understood our codependency. At first it was dangerous—we could have separated or divorced, but we stuck with it, and that broke the pattern of codependency."

Healing

David recognized the importance of not being dependent on Belinda. "From that point on, things started to get a lot better. I started to realize I could feel."

Belinda noted, "I was codependent . . . and many of the things a codependent spouse does will actually foster the addiction. I was dependent on him being dependent on me. I had to learn not to be."

They both noted, "We started to talk again."

Belinda: "That was the crux of it."

David: "At age fifty-two, I woke up—to myself, to the world, to God."

Belinda said, "I knew you would stop drinking because I knew you loved God."

David: "Those years were bad for the family. The effects on the children were not good, and I had become very clever at concealing my drinking. Even at work, they didn't know."

I noted, "You just didn't give up. Especially Belinda, she didn't give up."

David: "Neither one of us gave up."

Belinda: "It's important to be equitable here. You grow up with an alcoholic parent, and the chances are good that you are going to marry an alcoholic. But David mentioned codependence."

David: "We both struggled, each in our own way. Codependence is a system where one augments the other. Sometimes in a relationship when one isn't an alcoholic, they almost prefer that he / she be dependent."

Belinda: "It's familiar."

David: "When the spouse breaks the enabling behavior the couple depended upon, it can break the whole relationship, or it can lead to a new beginning. Our life has gone in different stages. Today is a completely different universe."

Belinda: "It's a much better universe. We're really enjoying each other and understand well what the other deals with."

I noted, "I'm going to propose to you that you survived because you started from genuine love and from conversation."

"Yes," they both said. "We were friends before we were lovers."

David: "People always told us that we balance each other. People saw what we didn't see. Each of us in terms of our own process, in relation to the marriage itself."

Belinda interjected, "There have always been a few people who would say, 'you guys do good together,' and I think those little remarks helped us. Certainly our belief in the teachings of Bahá'u'lláh have been immensely important to us."

David Erickson and Belinda Forsee have been married for almost fifty years, have three children, and five grandchildren. They recently completed a journey to Israel for Bahá'í pilgrimage, and spent several weeks in South Africa assisting the Bahá'í community in that country. Their story demonstrates the power of perseverance, and of hope.

Dealing with Conflict

Couples in long-term marriages somehow learned to discipline their emotional responses. For example, they generally learned not to "fly off the handle," in favor of slowing down and speaking to one another during stressful times. This evolution of a mature response appeared to indicate that changing one's attitude and responses takes time, and that time and patience are critical to the survival and joy of marriage.

Peter Brady even created his own personal "checklist" of advice for himself and others. He said,

Leave your ego behind. It can only destroy a marriage. Both people in a marriage are important, both have rights, both merit respect, both are human and less than perfect. One is not better or worse because of whatever reasons either of them manufactures to perpetuate their image of themselves vis-à-vis the rest of the world. Both are in the marriage to make it work; for this to happen, both must be allowed to be themselves. One may think that he / she is better educated, comes from a richer or more illustrious family, or has many other "qualities"—excuses?—for trying to get his or her way, but the truth is that these so-called "qualities" are unimportant.

Respect the other person as an equal, with different viewpoints, a different upbringing, education, values, dreams, hopes, fears, frustrations, needs, desires, and wants. Different is not wrong or evil, it is simply different. To make differences a source of argument will only bring about frustration.

Muguette Brady especially emphasized her appreciation for her husband's respect for her. She said that it was the most important factor in the sustenance of their marriage.

Her husband Peter also noted the importance of other virtues and listed them:

Honesty. No hidden agendas, no mind games where I expect my wife to behave a certain way, to do certain things just because she loves me, and therefore should know what I want without my having to say anything.

Trust in my spouse.

Forgiveness, both of myself and toward the rest of my family. To be able to put the past behind us and not use it in every argument forever after.

The Bradys both wrote to me about a very important aspect of their relationship: they felt that a sense of humor, shared laughter, had been really special to them. Peter listed his other themes briefly:

A sense of humor. The willingness and the need to laugh at ourselves.

A loving attitude toward my wife and the willingness to tell her and show her often. Just to say something once is not enough. Love needs to be demonstrated continually through gestures, actions, words.

Self-knowledge. Knowing my capacities and deficiencies, and accepting them. The deficiencies are to be worked on, to be lessened, overcome, or resolved; my capacities are also to be worked on to be developed to the utmost.

Courtesy

Courtesy within the family was, Coral and Ovidio Gomez noted, essential. Coral expressed the idea that courtesy was even more important within the family than towards strangers; after all, you have to live with the persons in the family!

The Slobodians also listed suggestions for nurturing the intimacy of marriage: educate one another sensually and sexually with tenderness and passion, cultivate a learning environment in the home that is flexible, creative, dynamic, and vision-based, and construct an inclusive home where other family, friends, and community contribute to the culture.

Again, I was struck by the verbs of process that are in use: educate, cultivate, construct. Marriage is being built.

Sandy continued, "Learn the art of mutual yielding, which is a delicate dance and not a score card."

So many other couples have emphasized similar convictions that I will let that one stand on its own. The ability to yield, and not keep score, seemed very important to many of the long-term marital partners.

There is also a belief system inherent within the Slobodians' philosophy:

Nourish the conviction that one's marital union has a reality, a creation brought about by a vow to the Creator of the Universe, and that it is an essential element of each member's reality.

Understand that the message is in the metaphor. A fortress is intended to protect against threatening forces, influences from within and without the relationship that will test the integrity of the union. We must therefore fortify it and not be shaken when we are tested.

Marriage and Family in the Afterlife

The idea that there is more than one world of God is not a significant change in the history of religious thought. Christianity and Islam call the world after death *heaven* or *hell*, and another religion uses the idea of *nirvana* to signify the world after death. In most cultures there is some kind of story about what happens to the soul after it leaves the physical world.

Regarding the world after physical death, the Bahá'í Faith believes that a married couple continues to be married even after both partners have passed beyond this world. This is the gist of spiritual connection. For instance, as noted in the epigraph to this chapter, 'Abdu'l-Bahá wrote that in an ideal marriage, the husband and wife "may enjoy everlasting unity throughout all the worlds of God." In other words, he is dispensing with the idea that husband and wife part at death. Their unity is more than just of this world. This way of thinking suggests, even further, the seriousness with which couples are meant to take the marriage bond.

When people are in the process of courtship, in ideal circumstances, there is little room for thinking that this may be only a temporary union. The Bahá'í perspective of "all the worlds of God" puts another spin on the importance of spirit: there is no "till death do us part" idea inherent in the marriage vow, and the union is not seen simply as a marriage of two individuals. Instead, it is seen as the beginning of a family whose relationships will endure beyond death, into the next world, where the marriage partners and their children will continue to live.

Dealing with the Loss of a Child

In dealing with loss during a marriage—such as that of a child—one theme that I found in these stories was the willingness to accommodate the other spouse's point of view. The flexibility of the partners seems very important to marital success, and it can provide a shelter for a married couple during a time of tragedy. Perhaps no one was more eloquent than Suzanne Schuurman in explaining this principle. She and Hubert had experienced the terrible grief of the loss of their son Tristan, about whose life she has written a moving biography. There is no doubt, however, that the deepest affection can be strained by life's circumstances.

Suzanne recounted,

Nadine, our oldest daughter, was away at University; Lisa, our youngest, had gone to live with a friend . . . and Hubert was away when Tristan fell into a coma. Hedda was my great strength and support. Hubert came home in time to hold Tristan as he expired, and he arranged for the funeral. That year Hedda left for a stint with "Crossroads in Africa," a youth organization dedicated to humanitarian service. The dog and I were alone in a house once overflowing with life. During school holidays I would fly out of Labrador and meet Hubert wherever he was filming. He was absorbed in his work, and I was still grieving and in a sort of shock. For the first time I could see why there are so many divorces in families that have lost a child. Men and women grieve differently.

Through all this sea of trials, my teaching work in the high school had kept me sane and focused. My husband enjoys traveling and being free to see new places. We had moved so often that I had not had time to establish myself in my profession, but this was beginning to change. So when Hubert talked about moving away from Labrador, it seemed like the last straw. I can still remember when he put it to me, how our ensuing discussion and the realization that I would have to sacrifice my professional development for the sake of our marriage was difficult. Yet, our marriage held.

The Schuurmans moved to Nova Scotia. Suzanne added, "I taught here and there and finished writing a book about our son Tristan. By this time another issue was looming on our horizon. Hubert wanted to move once more. This issue of frequently moving became more and more of a problem for me. By the time we had built a home in Nakusp, British Columbia, and Hubert agitated to move once again, it was without doubt the main point of disagreement between us.

But we are still together and still moving. To this day, we always try to think of the other person's point of view to work through any issue, even the emotional ones involving grief and loss."

Dealing with Illness

Diana and Don Dainty had been attracted to one another in part by their love of sports; both were fit, active, and under thirty years old when their two children arrived, only fifteen months apart. With the birth of the children, however, Diana became ill with a collagen disease that weakened her. Today, Diana has partially recovered from this illness but still experiences some challenges with her health.

When they married, Don and Diana had hoped that both of them would be able to work in their chosen professions. Instead, Diana's illness prevented her from working outside the home, as it left her tired and in pain. As with every married couple, they needed to develop consultative methods, or, as they put it, "Consultative methods had to be negotiated and established." One of Don's qualities, as Diana described it, is "single-mindedness," and his single-mindedness was a blessing for the family when Diana's illness persisted. Rather than being frustrated by this turn of events, the family rallied, and Don became a support to Diana in ways neither of them had anticipated. He ensured that his work could provide well for the family and assist Diana in every way possible to support her as she cared for their two children and coped with her disease.

Diana, for her part, also showed perseverance and steadfastness in accepting the situation. With two young children and health challenges, Diana could have become more and more isolated. She said, "It was difficult not to be able to go back to work as I had studied hard to become qualified as an occupational therapist and enjoyed the work." However, she noted that, in the Bahá'í community and in other areas, "There is lots to do."

Diana's skills, learned in university and hospital settings, were transferable to teaching arts and crafts to children, as well as starting a Learning Disabilities Association in Western Quebec for teachers and parents. Her consultation skills were brought to bear as chair of the school board committee for learning disabled students, as well as in cooperative parent endeavors to influence the school board to implement changes for the evaluation of the students. A sports program for pre-teens was also undertaken on Friday evenings, with considerable success.

In fact, as the children grew, the family became involved in different activities and traveled extensively both for work and for faith-related issues. The Daintys speak with enthusiasm about these activities. For example, later on, when the children were older, the Daintys agreed to do more joint activities, so when the Faith expressed the need for Don's participation, "both of us volunteered."

Such was the case for work to foster the Bahá'í Faith in Russia during the early '90s. They pointed out that it was "an opportunity not to be missed." The Iron Curtain had fallen and Russia had "opened its doors" to the world and welcomed our "citizen diplomats" into their inner circles. Sharing of employment and professional skills led to deeper questions about life in Canada and personal beliefs. The Daintys said, "The Russians had a great spiritual thirst, after seventy years of atheistic Communism, and they responded enthusiastically to Bahá'u'lláh's teachings. The pioneer families, including that of our daughter, her husband and two children, experienced many hardships and sacrifices, but we were also blessed with wonderful Russian friends and expanding experiences."

Don continues to admire Diana's courage and commitment to maintaining optimistic in the face of her illness. He said, "I admire Diana greatly for her fortitude. I don't think I'd have been able to cope so well with the constant challenge of illness as Diana has done."

In retrospect, the Daintys note that it is important to maintain a balance between family life and other activities, so that relationships can be nourished and human needs supported. Perhaps a husband and wife can find no greater support than themselves. As stated in the marriage tablet attributed to 'Abdu'l-Bahá, "Nourish continually the tree of your union with love and affection, so that it will remain ever green and verdant throughout all seasons and bring forth luscious fruits for the healing of the nations."[2]

Dealing with Anger

Coping with emotional responses to one's spouse was an important aspect of sustaining marriage for most couples. I had been wanting to know how people who were trying to work on the spiritual—as well as the emotional—aspects of marriage coped with the "negative" emotions such as anger, or perhaps jealousy. I found the variety of responses about how couples dealt with anger towards one another useful.

Ginny and Greg Kintz married young and have lived much of their lives as Bahá'í pioneers from the United States. They have two grown daughters. Ginny acknowledged the differences between her views and Greg's, and she offered the following perspective on disagreement: "We both realize that anger is an emotion born of self. No one can 'make me angry.' I allow myself to be angered. We have also learned that the best way to handle a situation when one of us is angry is to give that person space—some time to think, pray, and relax. We learned a long time ago not to have discussions or try to consult when one of us is angry. It is just not productive, and we end up saying things we don't really mean. This doesn't mean that we ignore problems—it's just that we know we can solve them much more constructively when we're not angry."

Sylvia de Vasquez also explored the idea of taking personal responsibility for one's feelings, after a conversation with her husband Yovanny:

> One thing he felt, and I agree, is that there is a necessary recognition that whatever you see in the other person, good or bad, is a reflection of yourself. This is both a very simple concept and very complicated in what it means in the practical, day-to-day getting along. Recognition of it is necessary to avoid blaming each other for what might be wrong. To use a practical example, Yovanny finds that if he starts getting frustrated with me because there are

clothes all over the house, he has to recognize that he is as much to blame for that as I am and just as responsible for doing something about it. Likewise, one time he agreed to do the dishes and wasn't doing them. After three days of the kitchen cleanup not getting done I couldn't stand it anymore and started washing the dishes. He came in and said to me, "You're just doing this to make me feel bad." I responded, quite honestly, "No, I'm doing the dishes because I can't stand the mess any more." He said, "So I shouldn't feel bad?" "If there would be a purpose to your feeling bad, you could, but there isn't, so don't." He shrugged, and that was that. It was not a guilt trip. I helped to make a mess of the kitchen too, there was no point to blaming him. Seeing yourself reflected in the other person has both spiritual implications as well as more basic ones that prevent you from pointing fingers at each other, which can only cause disunity.

Stuart North shared similar thoughts, particularly about the importance of finding a calm space from which to work out issues:

When we were first married, if I showed displeasure, frustration, or anger it would intimidate my wife. I didn't realize how it affected her. It sabotaged our efforts to communicate. In later years she resolved to be more forceful and not allow herself to be intimidated. For a number of years our exchanges, on occasion, were very heated and we were both upset for several days afterwards. Finally I decided not to get drawn into discussions about sensitive issues and to remain very dispassionate when discussing new issues or complaints. I now try to be very detached and not to take comments personally. As a result I feel very calm most of the time and try to focus on preserving family unity. Eventually we will learn to consult with one another!

Another friend also observed differences in style between her and her spouse. Tracy Khajavi noted the different ways that she and her husband Ali deal with emotion: "We deal with our emotions very differently. He is a man's man and doesn't show emotion very often; it takes quite a lot to shake his resolve. I know that if he gets mad at me he tells me right away (no guesswork there) and then simply forgets it. If I get mad I brew on it for several days and then finally say something. Even after I say something I tend to dwell a little too long on it afterward, it's irritating really. I find as time passes we are getting our dance steps a little more in time. I am getting better at voicing my feelings, and he doesn't always say something."

Karin Ferguson shares these observations: "If Ian and I had disagreements over the years . . . our inclination was to become very quiet and think about things for awhile . . . and then we would discuss the situation privately, away from our children. *Never* would we argue in front of our kids. They hear enough disunity outside, at school, and on the street without hearing it at home. Ian was raised this way and so was I. I would say that this was one of the best things in our marriage, keeping the parents' problems to ourselves—and never forgetting a sense of humor."

Bruce Filson noted the importance of keeping perspective, and he talked about his preference for how his wife, Margaret Bremner, coped with anger: "Anger happens. You can't take it personally. I yell and take it out on people. Margaret takes it out on things. Hers is better."

His wife noted, however, that Bruce's anger was rare: "Generally, neither of us is a particularly angry person. I get mad at objects that don't do what I want them to and then I bang them (doors, spoons, chairs, etc.) Bruce rarely gets angry. I think that mild, long-lasting (years) of postnatal depression is something our marriage—read 'Bruce'—had to cope with, and I commend him and am very grateful for his patience."

Creating an enduring marriage is an act, to some degree, of will, that includes subordinating personal predilections to a common goal. June Barrow shared thoughts about how she and Reggie had negotiated some of the challenges of differing viewpoints: "In recent years, we tend to ignore anger because we ultimately realize that it's what we call 'dead antsville,' referring to Bahá'u'lláh's injunction that this nether world is as important as the 'black in the eye of a dead ant' in comparison to all of eternity—in earlier years, we hadn't evolved to that level yet, and each of us was very hurt by the anger in the other and used to play the usual silly games.[3] I (June) used to feel that Reg's temper was bad for the children, but he's made a lot of progress on that in recent years, and the kids have survived it."

Changing one's point of view seems to be critical to the long-term happiness of a marriage. Robin Goertz, who became a Bahá'í in Africa, is married to Steven, a Buddhist. She shared an "epiphany" she had at one point during their marriage:

For twenty-five years now I have been slightly exasperated because Steven does not hang his damp bath towel up "properly" but rather hangs it in a slapdash fashion that leaves it wadded up on the towel bar. The consequence is that it does not then dry properly, tends to smell moldy and need washing sooner. I have resorted to various methods in my "mom and fellow earthling" toolkit, such as: demonstrating the proper method, explaining how wadding it up actually makes it smell scuzzy while offering a good strong whiff, demonstrating that it creates more laundry, correcting his method in front of him with a smiling reminder, correcting his method in front of him with a frown, offering to trade pet peeves—i.e., I would turn out the lights if he would hang the towel properly, or I would put the keys where they belong if he would hang the towel properly. And, of course, there are the whine, beg, and fuss methods, too.

I am amused by this story! Of such small habits, it seems, are relationships tested. Robin went on:

Twenty-five years and still the towel is wadded up, so I ask myself today, "What is this opportunity for me?" Suddenly, the light blinks, flashes, and beams directly at me. This is my chance to straighten his towel up, hopefully for the next twenty-five years, just as I have for the last twenty-five years. Only this time, I feel like doing it with love and appreciation for all the "behind the scenes" things he does for me—without whining, begging, or making a show of his actions.

This wadded towel—which I get to see sometimes three times a day in Jamaica where we sweat, swim, and shower frequently—is my silent cue, reminding me that I can appreciate people when they don't do things "my" way or the "logical" way; reminding me that I can love them not in spite of but, in fact, because of their seeming contrariness; reminding me that sometimes things I thought were big things are small things after all; reminding me how wonderfully stubborn I can be about an issue and that I should strive to make those issues the right ones; reminding me how absolutely silly I can be about an issue and that I should strive to let go of things sometimes; reminding me that others love me and I love them in spite of our flaws . . . and that that is a gift from God.

Robin said, "I can't wait for the towel to get wadded up next time. I am sure I will have my chance before bedtime tonight!"

A shift in perspective seems to mean a lot to how well we live with one another. How people respond to emotion seems also to be one of the elements of marriage that evolves. Marilee and David Rhody noted these changes over time; Marilee said of anger, "After twenty-eight years of marriage, we do not often become angry with one another. But, if we feel annoyed or disappointed, we talk about it together. We seek to please the other. If I am angry with others and cannot deal with it alone, I consult with David, whose wise perspective always soothes and helps me decide how to deal with the situation. Sometimes we pray together about a situation."

David added, "Early in our marriage my frustration and anger would bottle up and fester inside, which is the model I saw from my childhood. Slowly I learned to be more expressive of feelings like anger before they become big issues. As Marilee said, we do not often get angry with each other and when we do we discuss it."

Marilyn and Barry Smith approach angry feelings very similarly. They said, "We try to avoid anger by sharing our feelings and concerns before it reaches that point. Because we want to make each other happy, over the years we have learned what pleases or displeases each other. We both have high boiling points, and seldom have we reached them. Experience has also taught us that anger is almost always counterproductive."

I asked Parviz and Gillian how they dealt with being angry with one another. Parviz replied, "We try to resolve the difference before we go to bed. There has to be a resolution to the problem. Somebody has to break it up—somebody has to say I'm sorry, even if they think they are right and the other person is at fault."

Gillian acknowledged, "I get tearful when I'm angry. I don't throw things or swear; I get defensive."

Parviz laughed again, "I know exactly when I've ticked her off just by looking at her—after so many years together— the eyes are the mirrors of the soul—we know each other, she only has to come through the door and I know the signs. I don't like tears—this is a man thing—I don't give in to it, at least not on the surface."

"But I don't use it (tears) to get my own way," Gill said.

Parviz agreed, "Gill just stores things and crying unleashes it."

I asked about him.

"Oh," he said, "I get angry. I'm volatile, vocal. We're different in characters: Gill holds things, I don't—I can't, even professionally. I have had this in international conferences; I say what comes in my mind. I cannot hold it. But I have to 'pull teeth' with Gillian to get her to talk."

Gillian nodded agreement.

Parviz added, "The children know that I erupt but they also know when Gillian has had enough, when they have crossed the line."

Listening to each other, I could tell that they have learned to understand each other's moods and to communicate well. They each know that the other really cares. Such encouragement from one's spouse seems to be a vital component of marriage, and Parviz and Gill hold every second together as precious as they can. Both have endured life-threatening illnesses, and Parviz retired early. They take very good care of one another.

Peter Brady also expressed the importance of changing through tests. "We have changed together and independently. It sounds strange, but though we are very close, we are still individuals and therefore face different tests, in addition to those we face together."

He also linked their independent viewpoints to different cultural backgrounds. He said, "We come from two different cultures: she is French Canadian and I am American of Irish, Hispanic, and Polish heritage."

Peter expressed the idea that change is simply part of living:

Also, the simple fact of living with another human being has meant that we have both had to develop virtues, such as patience, the willingness to speak about what interests us, and consulting on the changes we face. My wife will be retiring soon and is going through what I call the "winding down phase." We talk about anything and everything, the large and the trivial. We approach tests differently. Me, I kick and scream and refuse to give in until I've spent my energy, while she is more willing to adapt and definitely accepts changes more quietly. But long years together have made us sensitive to the other's moods. One of the joys of being together for thirty-five years has been the ability to enjoy silence. We don't talk just for the sake of talking.

Patience and Working Together

The theme of patience for change seems to be very important to the longevity of these marriages. Bruce Filson captured this idea most concisely: "You have to adapt to the stages of marriage. Honeymoon passes to friendship to parenthood to old age. You have to roll with the punches."

Stuart North also expressed himself in terms of the work involved in marriage: "We have worked very hard to maintain our marriage because we love one another and both felt it was worth the effort. We also wanted to help our children to learn from our mistakes and to improve their own marriages in the process."

Consultation is key, and it evolves over time, as Stuart noted: "We recognize the importance of consultation but have not been very successful in using consultation in our discussions. Our children have had more success in this respect. Communication is probably our biggest challenge, and we continue to work on this aspect of our marriage."

Tracy Khajavi also said that she and her husband had to work at consultation: "We are still 'at work' in this area. I'm sure if we ever get it right, we'll be doing great. Because of the many different languages my husband speaks, we often don't take the time to really hear what the other person is saying. We are getting better at consultation as time passes."

Bill and Phoebe Anne Lemmon noted, "We have a successful marriage, but it has taken and still takes work."

People don't begin their marriages the same way, and it can take a very long time of working together in order for a couple to accomplish the changes they aspire to produce within their marriage.

Suzanne Schuurman also spoke about the differences that exist between marital partners:

Marriage is a lot of work. Since you cannot really change your partner there are only one's own attitudes and values to work on. When so many aspects of marriage work really well, it is possible to concentrate hard on one front. . . . I've had to work on myself a great deal to get rid of my longing to stay put somewhere, anywhere. Fortunately, detachment is often spoken of by Bahá'u'lláh. Lately I have come across a passage in the *Tablets of Bahá'u'lláh* that is like a gift from on high, "God willing thou mayest experience joy and radiance, gladness and exaltation in any city or land where thou mayest happen to sojourn."[4]

My husband is full of surprises and never boring. Most of our moves involved pioneering; they have exposed us to people and places that I would hardly have wanted to miss. Laughingly we refer to Hubert as "the Stradivarius"; he produces artistic works but is sensitive to drafts, wind and cold—the kind of sensitivity that makes us change tables in a restaurant and rooms in a hotel because of cold drafts or mysterious hums. By contrast I think of myself more as some percussion instrument that beats out the daily rhythm of life so that the Stradivarius can perform its virtuosity. My husband's "child" is very strong, providing a freshness of perception useful both in filmmaking and in writing. But it is also the kind of "child" that will loudly proclaim, "The Emperor has no clothes." Right now Hubert is writing a two volume fantasy; his imagination never ceases to astound and intrigue me. . . .

Suzanne spoke eloquently to the joys and sorrows of sustaining a long-term marriage that matures through trials into a thing of beauty:

We were married in 1959, so ours is a marriage of some duration. We rely on each other a great deal and are seldom apart now that work does not take Hubert far from home. Like any living relationship, our marriage has gone through many changes, and now that we are in our sunset years some of our old patterns of interaction are changing—I still like to cook nice meals and eat them by candlelight, but I am not as fastidious about cleaning anymore, and Hubert does all the vacuuming. He keeps our wood stove going, and while I cook and clean up he reads aloud. We have worked our way though many of the great classics and biographies. It provides a focus for our conversations.

To continue Suzanne's metaphor, it appears as though their orchestra is playing in tune. This was accomplished, as with many of these marriages, through hard work, based in love.

Like Suzanne, Maury Miloff spoke of the challenges, and the rewards, of marriage:

Probably, the single greatest factor has been commitment to marriage and children itself. How much of that is a positive commitment, and how much is fear of the consequences, I am not quite sure. Another factor is probably good financial management and reliable 'project' management. I think it would be good if each marriage had at least one person watching the finances to stave off bankruptcy. Having common values, such as how many material goodies we needed, also helped us —it reduced conflict in one more area.

What has worked: well, just what you always read about— the particular strengths of each person rising to the challenge and leading the couple out of the morass. In both our cases, we have gentle hearts and sensitive souls, and we were unable to withstand much conflict (disunity)—not only with each other but also with family and others. As a result, we often strove for patience and peace in all situations. Prayer and service to our faith kept us busy, and held us on the straight and narrow path, and made our petty problems seem relative. We both have a very strong interest in psychology and analytical dispositions, which kept us seeking a deeper truth about our natures and how we turned out the way we did. It greatly enhanced communication—particularly in our early stages. Humor also played an important role in our getting along, too.

If I had to summarize things—it is this: we never were inclined to take too many hard lines with each other. We are basically good people trying to get along without inordinate desires or destructive tendencies. . . .

Like Maury and Helen, Greg and Ginny Kintz have a positive philosophy about being gentle with one another in their marriage:

We both acknowledge that it has been work at times, but by and large our marriage is an easy one. What makes it so is the fact that we genuinely like each other and have fun together. Putting our faith first helps us not to take ourselves too seriously. There's also a great level of comfort from having stuck it out and been together so long— like the feeling of your favorite blanket or warm sweater. We "fit" together—we by and large know how the other person thinks, how he / she will react in a given situation, and his / her likes and dislikes.

Seeing Challenges as Blessings

Pierre Martel had also spoken about the challenges but equated challenge with blessings:

I think that, in many ways, one could say that marriage is the most difficult challenge one will ever face in life. It is the most demanding task. This is also commensurate with the greatness of this blessed institution and the greatness of the blessings attached to it. As such, it can only succeed if we put in a huge amount of effort. It is not as though there is a difficult period to pass through, and then everything is OK. Sure, the first years require that intensive changes and adaptations be made to one's life. However, it is a long process, and each period requires its own kind of contributions. I have said to my children that marriage is like one's individual development. I told them that our marriage took twenty-one years to become mature, so that they would not look at making marriage work as a short-term issue.

Maury Miloff offered these thoughts in summary: "I think a marriage, in order to thrive, needs, firstly, a lot of patience and tolerance, and also the ability to know when you better get some help. Honesty may be ideal, but learning how to keep your trap shut may be more practical when the only things you have to say are hurtful."

This is pretty good advice for anyone who is upset: take a deep breath, and wait! As Maury noted,

Taking responsibility for one's own unhappiness is essential. Otherwise, you mistakenly blame events and other people for your own failures. Courage is needed to break unhealthy molds you may find yourself in. Similarly, independence may be necessary when you have to do it on your own. I guess this comes down to the imperative of being really honest with your self. You can't run too far or too long from yourself without suffering horribly from not keeping faith with your own being.

As we move through life, eventfully and painfully, we inevitably learn something about who we are and what the positive and negative consequences of our thoughts, feelings and actions are. If we were to look at ourselves from the next world, the course here would probably seem like a zig-zagging obstacle course. But by going through these obstacles, we come to self-knowledge, and the teachings of religion have proven themselves to me over and over again as being a light to the path and a protection. Still, there is always a lot to go through, a lot of hard knocks, before the lessons really rub in and become sincerely yours.

I really liked this sense of mature ownership of feeling, which had been shared by many others as well: when there are challenges, it is important to start changing within ourselves.

Creating a Safe Harbor

Maury Miloff added his thoughts about marriage as being like a "safe harbor" that protected him during times of turmoil during his life:

Having a companion has provided me with serious ballast and balance, not to mention wisdom and succor in the midst of buffeting winds. Maybe this is because I am forced by the demands of life to work together with this person on the basics of the "spiritual good life." As a result, my marriage has always been a constant point of safety when I really needed it—a safe harbor. Our marriage partner is usually the lightning rod for our unhappiness and not adequately appreciated in the here and now, to say the least, but once we weather the storms, later at calmer moments of reflection we can always cherish the unspeakable, sacred gift of togetherness, burnished by the survival of all manner of tests.

Pierre Martel also spoke about the importance of personal accountability. "What has been very important for me in going through tests related to married life is two things. The first is the fear of God, and the second is looking at my own faults."

It is clear that we have to "own our own" responsibility for our feelings and our actions. Pierre added,

The love of God has been something of major importance in helping me express my love to my wife. In other words, I have tried to feel and express the similarity between loving God and loving her. This doesn't always work because God is perfect and Kamachee is not (and, obviously, I'm not either). Although the love of God is something so exalted that human love will never reach and compare with it, yet there are obvious similarities between the two. However, when times came for severe tests (and there were), it was the fear of God that held me back from doing stupid things (not that I never did). The way the Bahá'í writings speak about the importance of the institution of marriage is so clear that one cannot look lightly at being a cause of disruption to this sacred institution. That brings me to my second point.

Of course, whenever something goes wrong, we tend to put the blame on the other person. Sometimes, when I am frustrated about something my wife did or did not do, I tend to think "this is not fair, this is not just," and maybe I am even right in thinking that (and again, maybe not). However, on such occasions, I just need to look back at myself, at how many times, and in how many ways, I have been unfair to Kamachee, and how many times and in how many ways she has overlooked my small (or big) injustices, to become much more humble. I then turn to God and ask for forgiveness for having had such negative thoughts (or actions) towards the person He especially put for me in my life. As you see, faith plays an enormous part in keeping people together.

Manuel Marcial also wrote about the importance of his faith in his marriage. Manuel spoke with wonderful metaphors and some quotations from the Bahá'í teachings embedded as part of his language:

There is so much guidance in the [Bahá'í] writings of how humans should behave in all situations. It sometimes seems that the "fortress for well being" is constructed out of the logs, nails and bolts of everyday tests that confront all of us in our passage through this plane. Married life is a roller coaster where the high moments should always supersede the lows. It requires constantly looking at the good and overlooking the bad and being thankful for having been given the gift of your wife / husband. The Bahá'í writings state, "O God, increase my astonishment in Thee."[5] The soaring moments available to a man and a woman who have become the tutors of each others' souls must certainly be one of the salient heights of this earthly life.

Manuel closed his thoughts with his understanding of the image of the "fortress." He said, "What . . . Bahá'u'lláh brings to the fore is the certainty that underlying, occasionally irritating disagreements may be found in the thread of something precious, and these disagreements may rise phoenix-like from everyday moments. It helps to always have tucked away in a corner of the mind the knowledge of seeing 'the end in the beginning.'[6] Marriage is certainly the most wonderful milieu for spiritual growth, and it is a reflection of the progress and upward motion of the soul."

Manuel commented, too, on the joy of children also becoming attracted to the life of the spirit: "And then there is the Prince of Joys, the attribute of seeing your children become lovers of God. Not much can compare with that! In closing, it would seem to me that all too often we take having been created too easily for granted. Having had existence bestowed upon us, how magnificent it is that we came into the human kingdom."

My dear friend, Baxter Huston, who has been married to Anne for twenty years, also offered some of his quiet wisdom. His sense of humor always brings me joy. Here's Baxter, on marriage: "Don't take it too seriously, and don't look too deeply into the meanings, the values, and the worth of it. . . . Just live it and don't analyze it to death, or you'll lose sight of it. It can only be seen from the corner of the eye, and then only when you aren't trying to see it. Good luck with it, love."

Love

Any book about assisting marriages to endure, long and well and happily, can do little better than to end on a note of love. The couples here entered their marriages with hope, seeing the end in the beginning. They expected to spend the rest of their lives together, and in linking their spiritual destinies, to go on together through eternity. This required each of them to develop, to overcome challenges together, and to believe in one another. Many have raised children together, and some are grandparents; family life is important to all of them. They have humor, perseverance, honesty, and realism. These couples have working marriages that demonstrate faith in each other, faith in God and in their respective spiritual practices, and faith in their own abilities to build a lasting marriage.

I'd like to give the last word to Jameson Bond, a family friend who attended university, along with my father, in the 1950s, in Toronto, Canada. He wrote, in 2004, of his marriage to Gale: "I turn eighty-seven and Gale eighty-five, next month, and last July we celebrated our fifty-one years of marriage, and we're hoping for more to come."

CONCLUSION

O Thou kind Lord! Make Thou this marriage to bring forth corals and pearls. Thou art verily the All-Powerful, the Most Great, the Ever-Forgiving.

'Abdu'l-Bahá

I grew up listening to stories. My mother is a storyteller, with a great belly laugh and a delight in narration. She told stories about her past, growing up in the Depression years with her devout Baptist mother and her exuberant British father. She told stories about her youth and her sisters, along with their discovery of the Bahá'í Faith and what it meant to each of them. In their family of five, all four sisters, and eventually her mother, her mother's sister, and her father, accepted the Bahá'í teachings. My father and his sister also encountered and accepted these teachings, in the 1950s. When my mother married my father, in 1955, they married with love and attraction, confidence, and a deep and uniting faith.

I grew up hearing Mother's stories. My father must have heard each one innumerable times. Not too long ago, I asked Dad, "Don't you ever get tired of hearing the same stories, over and over again?"

His answer was simple, and took my breath away. He said, "I love hearing them, every time."

I grew up with a model of marriage that was, and is, a marriage of spirit. Their abiding faith taught my parents to consult, to commit themselves to each other and to their children, to welcome people from all cultures and walks of life into our home, and to believe, with profound conviction, in the inevitability of God's active blessings in their lives. My mother sang prayers to us, every day. My father talked with us about his faith and how to practice it in the "real world." Both wove love and faith as a part of a tapestry.

Their marriage was not perfect, but they tell me they consider that it has been an "easy" one. They shared their views on marriage and family life, when asked—and they were often asked by us and by friends—but mostly they showed us what marriage could be through the power of example. They encouraged us in our questions, and they were open, honest, and loving about challenges. When they had money problems, they consulted us. Whenever there were difficulties, the family prayed together. When they wanted to make a decision about something, they were inclusive: in 1965, they asked my two sisters and me whether we would like a little brother. We decided we would like that, and our family adopted a boy. Later, our two youngest sisters came along—surprise blessings from God.

As time passed, I became aware that what my parents were modeling for us was a gift. Not everyone enjoyed living in a family with the kind of parents we had. In fact, more and more, I became aware of how lucky we were, as more and more of my friends struggled with their parents' divorces, and then as our own generation got married, got divorced, and got married again. Throughout all the social changes that occurred around us, my father and my mother devoted themselves to each other, to our family, and to their faith.

They were not alone. Other couples of our acquaintance, old friends and new ones, provided models of happy marriages. Yet each marriage was apparently very different, and I began to realize that the ways for marriages to work well were many. I began to reflect about what gift I could offer our own children to hearten them about the possibility for marriages being happy in a social environment where each and every day they heard about another family which, for one reason or another, had been divided. The more divorce there was, the more there appeared to be a loss of hope.

I realized that children needed to know that happy marriages were possible. I could say to them, "Look at Grandma and Grandpa," and be sure that they had a model of a couple who enjoyed one another's company, through joy and sorrow, together in spirit. I could point to various couples, friends and acquaintances, and speak about how they appeared to be happy. I was also very grateful that our children were growing up in a home where my husband and I continued to love each other deeply.

Yet I also wanted to understand what it was that made such marriages not only survive, but in many cases, flourish. It was one thing to see that there were people around who had been married to one another for a long time, and were still happy together; it was another to be able to try and put my finger on what made the difference between couples who were committed to one another and those who, in the face of circumstance, separated and divorced. So I began to ask questions. First, I asked people I knew fairly well, since the questions were quite personal. As I heard their answers, I realized that I was hearing stories that were precious, and that I was receiving the wonderful gift of glimpsing people's lives through their willingness to share. I was hearing stories that were wise, caring, thoughtful, sometimes funny, and sometimes sad. The most grievous were those where I heard those couples relate their pain at losing a child. I found it particularly inspiring that such trials increased the devotion of the couple to one another. As I heard more stories, I began to see certain currents running throughout them.

I had started with asking people in my faith community about their marriages, and the significance of spiritual practice as a uniting factor certainly emerged as being of tremendous importance to most of the couples. Spirituality alone, however, was not enough to understand why these marriages worked. The partners walked the spiritual path with practical feet. Often, they learned to respect, consult, and pray about everything: finances, raising children, and communication styles were among the areas of continual growth. Each couple had different ways of dealing with emotional responses, work, faith, and tests and difficulties, yet each couple was deeply committed to making their marriage work.

As I began collecting stories, I told my father I was thinking of writing a book about happy marriages. He told me it would be difficult to get people to talk about the subject honestly enough for it to be useful. He laughed, "Especially if you want them to talk about sex!"

I agreed that it would be a challenge, but the stories I had already heard—both from growing up with my parents and from starting to ask questions of other couples—had convinced me that there were still more stories to be heard. I suspected that the more I heard, the more hope I would have, and the more hope I could offer to our children.

Like my father listening to my mother's stories, I found that the stories became richer and fuller the more I heard them. I began receiving wonderful letters from people I hardly knew, and some whom I had never met, sharing glimpses of their lives, together with the delights and challenges they had endured. Friends would write and say, "You really should ask this couple. They have a great marriage!" Thus, this book grew. It could have continued to grow; there are so many wonderful stories! My favorite quote from the writings of 'Abdu'l-Baha is found in chapter 2. It reads, "Each sees in the other the Beauty of God reflected in the soul, and finding this point of similarity, they are attracted to one another in love." I cannot think of a better definition for spiritual love, and I am deeply grateful for the generosity of those who have taken the time to share their stories with me.

I hope that these stories have offered you a glimpse of the strength in marriages grounded in loving and spiritual partnership, replete with joy as families learn and grow together, and that they enrich your sense of hopefulness about the wonderful possibilities of marriage, as they have done for me.

I hope you find your own stories.

CONTRIBUTORS

June and Reginald Barrow were married on October 15, 1978, in Laguna Beach, California. They have two sons, Adam and Isaac, and three grandchildren. The family served as Bahá'í pioneers for over twelve years in Cameroon, West Africa, then moved to Canada with their adopted daughter, Susan, where June accepted a position as vice principal of the Maxwell International Bahá'í School. Upon leaving Canada the Barrows went to Swaziland, in southern Africa, where June passed away.

David and Carol Bowie married in February 1955 and have three children in this world and three in the next. They have twelve grandchildren and one great-grandson.

Peter and Muguette Brady recently celebrated their thirty-fifth anniversary. They have two grown sons, both of whom have chosen to be Bahá'ís. Muguette is a French-Canadian, and Peter was born in New York City and grew up in upstate New York. Since becoming Bahá'ís they have lived in several parts of Quebec.

David and Haodan Mary Brown celebrated their fifth wedding anniversary recently and are expecting their first child. David is Canadian and Haodan is from China.

Bruce K. Filson and Margaret Bremner have been married since 1978 and are the parents of three girls. Bruce is a writer and poet who continues to support the family as a teacher, salesman, translator, and editor. Margaret has pursued her career in art, focusing for the past decade on mandala imagery (see http://www.artistsincanada.com/bremner).

Don and Diana Dainty were raised in an area north of Toronto and were married in 1956. They have two grown children and two granddaughters.

Steve and Andrea Doran were married in 1977. They have five children and one grandchild, with another on the way.

Cheryl Kinchen and Gordon Epp met in Saskatoon in 1972 and married in 1973. Parents of three sons, the last several years have been devoted to caring for Salim and Angus, who were living with muscular dystrophy. Salim passed away at age 11, and Gord stays at home as a caregiver for Angus, now 18. Seamus, the eldest, is married to Sonja.

Edward Epp has been married to Leanne for over twenty years, and they have two children, Amelia and Nathaniel. Ed is a talented visual artist whose work can be viewed at http://www.edwardepp.com/.

Belinda and David Erickson have been married for almost fifty years. They have three grown children and several grandchildren, and they reside in Canada.

Karin and Ian Ferguson have been married for over fifty years and have been Bahá'ís for forty. Throughout their marriage, Karin and Ian have moved, at last count, twenty-six times. They have three children and six grandchildren who live in different parts of Canada and the United States.

Robin Goertz has been married to Steven Goertz for twenty-seven years, and they are the parents of Hunter, Hans, and Mackenzie. Robin is originally from Missouri but encountered the Bahá'í faith while living in Lesotho. Her husband Steven is a Buddhist.

Ovidio and Coral Gomez met and married in Haifa, Israel, and celebrated their fifteenth anniversary in October 2005. They have five children. They have been Bahá'í pioneers in either Honduras or Belize for most of their lives together, and they are now residing in northern Canada.

Nahid and Rick Gordon have shared thirty-seven years of marriage together. They have two sons and one grandson.

Ann and David Hall have been married for over thirty years, spending twenty-five of those years in Papua New Guinea, where they raised four of their own children and helped to raise four or five Papua New Guinean youth. The Halls are now back in the United States, living in Tennessee.

Baxter and Anne Huston live in northwestern British Columbia. They have been married for over twenty years and have two daughters.

Wendy James and Bernie Benoit have been married for over two decades and have two grown children and one Haitian son-in-law. They all continue to serve the Bahá'í Faith from home in Ottawa, Ontario.

Ali and Tracy Khajavi live in Quebec, Canada. Ali is from a Muslim background and grew up in Iran. Tracy is from a Christian background and grew up in Canada. Both have become Bahá'ís. They met in British Columbia, have been married for over a decade, and have two boys.

Ahkivgak Kiana (Luke Baumgartner) comes from two cultures, American Caucasian and Inupiat, one of the Alaskan First Nations tribes. He is now divorced but shared views on step-parenting and its effect on marriages, as well as observations of his grandparents' and parents' marriages, and how the Bahá'í teachings influenced them.

Greg and Ginny Kintz have been married since 1977 and have two adult daughters. Originally from Michigan, they have assisted in the development of Bahá'í communities in both East and West Africa and rural South Carolina. They currently live in East Timor.

Louise Profeit and Bob LeBlanc have been married for twenty-four years. They met in the Yukon and currently reside in Wakefield, near Ottawa. Bob assisted in raising Louise's children from her first marriage and is now helping raise her grandson Alexander.

Phoebe Anne and Bill Lemmon were married in March 1972, a second marriage for both. Phoebe Anne was a widow with three children; Bill had two adopted children who lived with his first wife. They are in their 70s, living happily in a Bahá'í community in British Columbia.

Bea and Clyde MacTavish have been married for almost fifty years. Residents of Western Quebec, they have three grown children and also enjoy their beloved grandchildren.

Currently living in Sydney, Australia, Mariette and Ho-San Leong celebrated their thirty-sixth wedding anniversary at the end of 2005. Their lifetime "loving, happy marital adventure" took them to Papua New Guinea, where they lived for over twenty years. Two of their four children were born there, and they adopted their daughter Seff, who comes from historic Madina. They are proud grandparents to Seff and Zia's two children and also to Tivien, the daughter of Seff's older sister. In October 2005, they added a fourth grandchild to their growing family. Their eldest daughter Mei-Ling is married to Darwin Price, and after a period of time in Nashville, Tennessee, they have returned to Australia, where they are expecting their first child. Mariette and Ho-San's last two grown-up children are living at home: Kim, their only son, and Fei-Lee, the youngest daughter, who is in the last semester of her university studies.

Manuel J. Marcial and his wife have been married for over forty years and have three children.

Pierre and Kamachee Martel met in Cameroon in 1975 and married in 1976. Their son Olinga lives in South Africa with his beautiful African wife and their son. Their daughter Rani Carmel pursues her studies in Canada.

In 2005 Helen de Marsh and Maury Miloff celebrated their twenty-seventh wedding anniversary in Bangladesh. Maury was raised in Montreal, Winnipeg and New York by devoted Jewish parents, the children of immigrants who fled persecution in Europe. Helen was raised in Toronto and the Maritimes. Together, they have raised three globe-trotting children in Canada, Uganda, Indonesia, Ethiopia and Bangladesh. These are Alexander (Ali), Zachary, and Hayley Miloff.

Susan Eghrari Moraes was born in Rio de Janeiro, Brazil, of Persian background, and graduated with a degree in architecture and urbanism in 1983. She moved with her husband Tunico to the center west region of Brazil in 1985, where their three children were born. Presently, she is taking her masters degree in sustainable planning.

Parviz Mottahed was born in Shiraz, Iran and went to the UK for his post-secondary education in 1958. He met his wife Gillian while at the University of Leeds. Two years later they were married and started continent hopping. Gillian quit working outside the home when their first child, Dara, arrived, and she continued to be a homemaker when Parisa and Fiona arrived and the three children were at home. The family immigrated to Canada in 1982 and are happily retired in Ottawa, close to their three children and six grandchildren.

Ron and Edna Nablo were married in 1955, have six children, twenty-one grandchildren, one great-grandchild, and another great-grandchild on the way. Both were of Christian background but chose the Bahá'í Faith in the 1950s, and they were married in one of the first Bahá'í ceremonies in Canada. Their story and their conversations about marriage and family life inspired the idea for this book. They are the beloved parents of the author.

Stuart North and Adelie (née Perreault) had a Bahá'í wedding ceremony in Vancouver, BC, on March 26, 1971. The couple has four children and three grandchildren. They both became Bahá'ís a few months after their marriage in 1971 and spent many years as Bahá'í pioneers to Haiti before returning to northern Saskatchewan.

Hélène Wallingford Panalaks and Dr. Thavil (Tony) Panalaks were married for over forty years before Tony's death early in 2006. Their marriage was one dedicated to communication across cultures: Hélène was born into a French-Canadian Christian family, and Tony was a Thai Buddhist. Both became Bahá'ís. Although they had no children of their own, they mentored and nurtured many young people from extended family and friends.

Arnold and Junia Perreault were married in Haiti, Junia's home, almost twenty years ago. Arnold is stepfather to Franz, Junia's son from her first marriage, and they are parents to Calixte, who, like Junia, is HIV positive. The family resides in St. Brieux, Saskatchewan, Canada.

Bibiane and Emile Perreault celebrated sixty years of marriage in 2005. French-Canadians from Saskatchewan, they have farmed in small town Hoey, near Prince Albert, all their lives, raising seven children in the Catholic faith. Six of their children chose to be Bahá'ís. They have many grandchildren.

David and Marilee Rhody celebrated their thirtieth wedding anniversary in July 2006. They are parents of two children who were both born in Mali, West Africa, where David and Marilee served as Bahá'í pioneers for over thirteen years. Their daughter has recently married.

Michael and Elizabeth Rochester were married in 1958. They have three children and two grandchildren. The first three members of the family were each born in a different country: Scotland, Canada, and the United States of America. They pioneered to Newfoundland in 1967 and continue to live there. They both served on the National Spiritual Assembly of Canada and also on a number of Local Spiritual Assemblies. They currently serve on the Bahá'í Council of the Atlantic Provinces.

Suzanne was born in Poland and Hubert Schuurman in Holland. They have been married since 1959. Their marriage was enriched by four children, and they are now grandparents.

Pat and Sandy Slobodian met in high school in northern British Columbia and declared their belief in Bahá'u'lláh together. Their children are Katrina, Mayana, and Quinn (in alphabetical order). Their extended family now includes many Bahá'ís, including the family matriarch, Stella. They make their home in Victoria, British Columbia, and welcome people from all walks of life.

Barry and Marilyn Smith celebrated their thirty-third anniversary recalling their marriage on April 1, 1972. They are parents of three daughters, one of whom has passed away. They left the United States to pioneer to Puerto Rico from 1975 to 1979, then spent a year in Ann Arbor, Michigan before leaving for Honduras, where they lived from 1980 to 2000. They currently live in Nicaragua.

On September 1, 1973, Pam Watts and Jeff Stellick were married in Weyburn, Saskatchewan. They have two children, Erin and Lael, and now live in Quebec.

Margaret and William Varner were married in Maryland in 1979. Parents of five children, eleven grandchildren, and two great-grandchildren, with more coming, they have served the Bahá'í Faith in a number of places, including six years at Maxwell International Bahá'í School as dorm parent supervisors, taking care of a considerable extended family. They now live in Georgia, where they are both working and pursuing their Master's degrees.

Yovanny and Sylvia Vasquez met at a Bahá'í workshop in Honduras, Yovanny's home country. They were married in February of 1994. For eleven years they served as pioneers in Belize, after which they moved to Canada, Sylvia's country of origin. Yovanny was trained in the Ruhi institute process—a Bahá'í educational program—in Colombia and spent much of his adult life teaching the Bahá'í Faith in the jungles of Honduras before meeting Sylvia. They reside with their three daughters in northern Alberta.

Janis and Leo Zrudlo have been married for forty-five years and have lived in Quebec City for over thirty. They have two daughters and seven grandchildren, and they presently divide their time between Gatineau, Quebec, and Cyprus, where they have been Bahá'í pioneers for the past ten years.

NOTES

Introduction

The epigraph for the Introduction is from 'Abdu'l-Bahá, *Selections*, 84.2.

1. Marḏíyyih Nabíl Carpenter, "Commemoration of the Twenty-Fifth Anniversary of 'Abdu'l-Bahá's Visit to America," in *The Bahá'í World: A Biennial International Record, Volume VII, 1936–1938*, comp. National Spiritual Assembly of the Bahá'ís of the United States and Canada (New York: Bahá'í Publishing Committee, 1939), p. 219; Bahá'u'lláh, *Seven Valleys*, p. 15.

2. Bahá'u'lláh, in *Bahá'í Prayers*, p. 118.

3. 'Abdu'l-Bahá, *Selections*, 84.4.

1 / Spiritual Foundations and Emotional Development

The epigraph for chapter 1 is from 'Abdu'l-Bahá, *Selections*, 84.4.

1. Ibid., 86.1.

2. From a talk ascribed to 'Abdu'l-Bahá by Mirzá Aḥmad Sohrab. The full text can be found at http://www.geocities.jp/oneworld_international/library/ab/marry_e.htm.

3. 'Abdu'l-Bahá, *Selections*, 94.2.

4. J. E. Esslemont, *Bahá'u'lláh and the New Era*, p. 82.

5. Bahá'u'lláh, in *Bahá'í Prayers*, p. 118.

6. 'Abdu'l-Bahá, *Selections*, 92.1.

7. From a talk ascribed to 'Abdu'l-Bahá by Mirzá Aḥmad Sohrab. The full text can be found at http://www.geocities.jp/oneworld_international/library/ab/marry_e.htm.

8. 'Abdu'l-Bahá, *Paris Talks*, 58.7.

2 / Love

The epigraph for chapter 2 is from 1 Corinthians 13:1–13, American Standard Version.

1. 'Abdu'l-Bahá, *Paris Talks*, 58.7.

2. 'Abdu'l-Bahá, *Selections*, 92.1.

3. Antoine de Saint-Exupéry, *Wind, Sand, and Stars.* Harcourt Brace Javanovich, New York, 1967, ch. 9. See Columbia World of Quotations, at http://www.bartleby.com/66/11/47911.htm.

4. 'Abdu'l-Bahá, *Paris Talks*, 6.7.

3 / Family and Consent

The epigraph for chapter 3 is from Bahá'u'lláh, Kitáb-i-Aqdas, ¶65.

1. 'Abdu'l-Bahá, *Selections*, 85.1.

2. Letter written on behalf of Shoghi Effendi to the National Spiritual Assembly of the United States and Canada, October 25, 1947, in *Lights of Guidance*, no. 1235.

3. Letter from the Universal House of Justice to the National Spiritual Assembly of the Bahá'ís of New Zealand, *Messages from the Universal House of Justice: 1963–1986*, 272.5e.

4. 'Abdu'l-Bahá, *Selections*, 114.1.

4 / Chastity and Sex

The epigraph for chapter 4 is from 'Abdu'l-Bahá, quoted in extracts from *The Bahá'í Teachings Discouraging Divorce*, in *Lights of Guidance*, no. 1306.

1. Letter of the Universal House of Justice to an individual Bahá'í, February 6, 1973, in *Lights of Guidance*, no. 1209.

2. Bahá'u'lláh, *Gleanings*, 52.2.

3. Bertrand Russell, *The Autobiography of Bertrand Russell*, p. 3.

4. Adib Taherzadeh, *Revelation of Bahá'u'lláh*, 1:3; Bahá'u'lláh, Kitáb-i-Íqán, ¶213.

5. Bahá'u'lláh, Kitáb-i-Íqán, ¶216.

6. Sarah McLachlan, "Possession," compact disc, *Fumbling Towards Ecstasy*, Arista 18725.

7. From a letter of Shoghi Effendi to an individual Bahá'í, September 28, 1941, in *Lights of Guidance*, no. 1212.

5 / Children

The epigraph for chapter 5 is from a talk ascribed to 'Abdu'l-Bahá by Mirzá Aḥmad Sohrab. The full text can be found at http://www.geocities.jp/oneworld_international/library/ab/marry_e.htm.

6 / Financial and Cultural Issues

The epigraph for chapter 6 is from a letter written on behalf of Shoghi Effendi, in "Family Life," *The Compilation of Compilations*, 1:398–99.

1. 'Abdu'l-Bahá, *Promulgation of Universal Peace*, p. 150.

2. Attributed to 'Abdu'l-Bahá. Taherzadeh, *Revelation of Bahá'u'lláh*, 4:217.

3. The Báb, in *Bahá'í Prayers*, p. 150.

7 / Through all the Worlds of God

The epigraph for chapter 7 is from 'Abdu'l-Bahá, *Selections*, 86.2.

1. 'Abdu'l-Bahá, *Bahá'í Scriptures*, p. 504.

2. From a talk ascribed to 'Abdu'l-Bahá by Mirzá Aḥmad Sohrab. The full text can be found at http://www.geocities.jp/oneworld_international/library/ab/marry_e.htm.

3. Bahá'u'lláh, *Summons of the Lord of Hosts*, "Súriyi-i-Haykal," ¶156.

4. Bahá'u'lláh, *Tablets of Bahá'u'lláh*, p. 175.

5. Bahá'u'lláh, *Seven Valleys*, p. 34.

6. Ibid., p. 15.

Conclusion

The epigraph for the Conclusion is from 'Abdu'l-Bahá, in *Bahá'í Prayers*, pp. 119–20.

BIBLIOGRAPHY

Works of Bahá'u'lláh

Gleanings from the Writings of Bahá'u'lláh. Translated by Shoghi Effendi. Wilmette, IL: Bahá'í Publishing, 2005.

The Kitáb-i-Aqdas: The Most Holy Book. 1st pocket-size ed. Wilmette, IL: Bahá'í Publishing Trust, 1993.

The Kitáb-i-Íqán: The Book of Certitude. Translated by Shoghi Effendi. Wilmette, IL: Bahá'í Publishing, 2003.

The Seven Valleys and the Four Valleys. New ed. Translated by Ali-Kuli Khan and Marzieh Gail. Wilmette, IL: Bahá'í Publishing Trust, 1991.

The Summons of the Lord of Hosts: Tablets of Bahá'u'lláh. Wilmette, IL: Bahá'í Publishing, 2006.

Tablets of Bahá'u'lláh revealed after the Kitáb-i-Aqdas. Compiled by the Research Department of the Universal House of Justice. Translated by Habib Taherzadeh et al. Wilmette, IL: Bahá'í Publishing Trust, 1988.

Works of 'Abdu'l-Bahá

Paris Talks: Addresses Given by 'Abdu'l-Bahá in Paris in 1911. Wilmette, IL: Bahá'í Publishing, 2006.

The Promulgation of Universal Peace: Talks Delivered by 'Abdu'l-Bahá during His Visit to the United States and Canada in 1912. Compiled by Howard MacNutt. 2nd ed. Wilmette, IL: Bahá'í Publishing Trust, 1982.

Selections from the Writings of 'Abdu'l-Bahá. Compiled by the Research Department of the Universal House of Justice. Translated by a Committee at the Bahá'í World Center and Marzieh Gail. Wilmette, IL: Bahá'í Publishing Trust, 1997.

Works of the Universal House of Justice

Messages from the Universal House of Justice, 1963–1986: The Third Epoch of the Formative Age. Compiled by Geoffrey W. Marks. Wilmette, IL: Bahá'í Publishing Trust, 1996.

Compilations

Bahá'u'lláh, the Báb, and 'Abdu'l-Bahá. *Bahá'í Prayers: A Selection of Prayers Revealed by Bahá'u'lláh, the Báb, and 'Abdu'l-Bahá.* Wilmette, IL: Bahá'í Publishing Trust, 2002.

Bahá'u'lláh, the Báb, 'Abdu'l-Bahá, Shoghi Effendi, the Universal House of Justice. *The Compilation of Compilations: Prepared by the Universal House of Justice 1963–1990.* 2 vols. Australia: Bahá'í Publications Australia, 1991.

Bahá'u'lláh and 'Abdu'l-Bahá. *Bahá'í Scriptures: Selections from the Utterances of Bahá'u'lláh and 'Abdu'l-Bahá.* Edited by Horace Holley. New York: Bahá'í Publishing Committee, 1928.

Hornby, Helen, comp. *Lights of Guidance: A Bahá'í Reference File.* New ed. New Delhi, India: Bahá'í Publishing Trust, 1994.

Other Works

Carpenter, Mar'iyyih Nabil, "Commemoration of the Twenty-Fifth Anniversary of 'Abdu'l-Bahá's Visit to America," in *The Bahá'í World: A Biennial International Record, Volume VII, 1936–1938.* Compiled by the National Spiritual Assembly of the Bahá'ís of the United States and Canada. New York: Bahá'í Publishing Committee, 1939.

de St. Exupéry, Antoine, *Wind, Sand, and Stars.* New York: Harcourt Brace Javanovich, 1967.

Esslemont, J. E. *Bahá'u'lláh and the New Era: An Introduction to the Bahá'í Faith.* Wilmette, IL: Bahá'í Publishing, 2006.

McLachlan, Sarah. "Possession," in *Fumbling Towards Ecstasy.* Compact disc, Arista, 1993.

Russell, Bertrand. *The Autobiography of Bertrand Russell.* New York: Routledge, 1998.

Taherzadeh, Adib. *The Revelation of Bahá'u'lláh: Baghdád 1853–63.* Rev. ed. Oxford: George Ronald, 1976.

———. *The Revelation of Bahá'u'lláh: Mazra'ih & Bahjí 1877–92.* Oxford: George Ronald, 1987.

Index

Bahá'í Publishing
and the Bahá'í Faith

Bahá'í Publishing produces books based on the teachings of the Bahá'í Faith. Founded nearly 160 years ago, the Bahá'í Faith has spread to some 235 nations and territories and is now accepted by more than five million people. The word "Bahá'í" means "follower of Bahá'u'lláh." Bahá'u'lláh, the founder of the Bahá'í Faith, asserted that he is the Messenger of God for all of humanity in this day. The cornerstone of his teachings is the establishment of the spiritual unity of humankind, which will be achieved by personal transformation and the application of clearly identified spiritual principles. Bahá'ís also believe that there is but one religion and that all the Messengers of God—among them Abraham, Zoroaster, Moses, Krishna, Buddha, Jesus, and Muḥammad—have progressively revealed its nature. Together, the world's great religions are expressions of a single, unfolding divine plan. Human beings, not God's Messengers, are the source of religious divisions, prejudices, and hatreds.

The Bahá'í Faith is not a sect or denomination of another religion, nor is it a cult or a social movement. Rather, it is a globally recognized independent world religion founded on new books of scripture revealed by Bahá'u'lláh.

Bahá'í Publishing is an imprint of the National Spiritual Assembly of the Bahá'ís of the United States.

For more information about the Bahá'í Faith,
or to contact the Bahá'ís near you, visit
http://www.bahai.us/
or call
1-800-22-UNITE

Other Books Available
from Bahá'í Publishing

Bahá'u'lláh and the New Era:
An Introduction to the Bahá'í Faith
J. E. Esslemont
$14.00 / $17.00 CAN
Trade Paper
1-931847-27-4

Bahá'u'lláh and the New Era stands as the very best general introductory book about the Bahá'í Faith of its time. Having been translated into some sixty-seven languages, it remains today the most widely known and most used textbook of the Bahá'í Faith. In this compact work, Esslemont comprehensively yet succinctly sets forth the teachings of Bahá'u'lláh, the faith's Prophet and Founder. He outlines the early history of the faith, explains its theology, incorporates extracts from its scripture, and provides information on Bahá'í spiritual practices. Essential reading for students of comparative religion.

Faith, Physics, and Psychology:
Rethinking Society and the Human Spirit
John Fitzgerald Medina
$17.00 / $20.00 CAN
Trade Paper
1-931847-30-4

In *Faith, Physics, and Psychology: Rethinking Society and the Human Spirit*, John Medina explores new developments in three different but complementary movements—physics, psychology, and religion—that reflect a new understanding of what it means to be human. Written in the style of Fritjof Capra's *The Turning Point: Science, Society, and the Rising Culture*, with one critical difference: Medina includes discussions regarding the role of religion and spirituality in building a new society. Despite the progress of Western civilization in economic, scientific, and other areas, a lack of corresponding progress with respect to spiritual life has left much of society feeling disoriented and unbalanced. Medina's insight sheds light on ways to address this imbalance. The ultimate goal of this examination is to present a path toward a prosperous global civilization that fulfills humanity's physical, psychological, and spiritual needs.

Paris Talks:
Addresses Given by 'Abdu'l-Bahá in 1911
'Abdu'l-Bahá
$12.00 / $15.00 CAN
Trade Paper
1-931847-32-0

This collection of inspiring and uplifting talks documents an extraordinary series of public addresses 'Abdu'l-Bahá gave on his historic trip to the West in the early twentieth century. Despite advanced age and poor health, he set out from Palestine in 1911 on a momentous journey to Europe and North America to share the teachings and vision of the Bahá'í Faith with the people of the West. Addressing such subjects as the nature of humankind, the soul, the Prophets of God, the establishment of world peace, the abolition of all forms of prejudice, the equality of women and men, the harmony of science and religion, the causes of war, and many other subjects, 'Abdu'l-Bahá spoke in a profound yet simple manner that transcended social and cultural barriers. His deep spiritual wisdom remains as timely and soul-stirring as it was nearly a century ago. 'Abdu'l-Bahá, meaning *Servant of the Glory*, is the title assumed by 'Abbás Effendi (1844–1921)—the eldest son and appointed successor of Bahá'u'lláh, the Prophet and Founder of the Bahá'í Faith. A prisoner since the age of nine, 'Abdu'l-Bahá shared a lifetime of imprisonment and exile with his father at the hands of the Ottoman Empire. He spent his entire life in tireless service to, and promotion of, Bahá'u'lláh's cause and is considered by Bahá'ís to be the perfect exemplar of the Faith's teachings.

The Summons of the Lord of Hosts:
Tablets of Bahá'u'lláh
Bahá'u'lláh
$14.00 / $17.00 CAN
Trade Paper
1-931847-33-9

The Summons of the Lord of Hosts brings together in one volume several major letters written by Bahá'u'lláh, prophet and founder of the Bahá'í Faith. In these magnificent documents he invites the monarchs and leaders of his time to accept the basic tenets of his Faith, sets forth the nature of his mission, and establishes the standard of justice that must govern the rule of those entrusted with civil authority. Written between 1868 and 1870, the letters call upon leaders of the East and West to accept Bahá'u'lláh's teachings on the oneness of God, the unity of all religions, and the oneness of humanity. Among the leaders specifically addressed are Napoleon III, Czar Alexander II, Queen Victoria, Náṣiri'd-Dín Sháh, and Pope Pius IX. A vitally important resource for those interested in the scripture and history of the world's great religions.

The Journey of the Soul:
Life, Death, and Immortality
Compiled by Terrill G. Hayes, Betty J. Fisher, Richard A. Hill, Terry J. Cassiday
$14.00 / $17.00 CAN
Trade Paper
1-931847-28-2

Drawing on extracts from Bahá'í scripture, *The Journey of the Soul* explains the purpose of material and spiritual existence and encourages us to live in a way that is mindful of the spiritual realities of this world and the next. The journey begins and ends with some of the weightiest questions we can pose about our reality as human beings: What is the purpose of life? What is death? How do we attain true happiness? What is the soul, and how does it develop? What is the nature of the next world? Will we know and recognize our loved ones? Each chapter includes comforting prayers and meditations.

The Heroic Female Spirit:
A Collection of Tales
Phyllis K. Peterson
$14.00 / $17.00 CAN
Trade Paper
1-931847-29-0

Myths and legends have traditionally been the domain of men and boys. The gallant hero is almost always male. In this spirited collection of stories, author, performer, and storyteller Phyllis Peterson places women and girls at the center of each story—discovering their inner gifts, defying restrictive customs, and creating peace between seemingly implacable foes. These young women demonstrate that heroic qualities are not the exclusive domain of young men and boys but are human qualities that can be found within each of us, regardless of gender. Each tale shows a young woman making a difference by acting fearlessly to improve the world around her.

The Power of Prayer:
Make a Joyful Noise
Pamela Brode
$15.00 / $18.00 CAN
Trade Paper
1-931847-10-X

Faced with raising two children with disabilities and the loss of her eyesight, Brode experienced seemingly insurmountable hardships in her personal life. Through her discovery of the power of prayer, she rose to meet the challenges facing her family with remarkable strength and fortitude. Inspired by her personal experiences, Brode set out to collect stories from others who had firsthand experience with the transformative power of prayer. The result is a heartwarming collection that demonstrates how prayer can assist us in overcoming individual challenges and in effecting social change.

Lights of the Spirit:
Historical Portraits of Black Bahá'ís
in North America 1898–2000
Gwendolyn Etter-Lewis and Richard Thomas, Editors
$17.00 / $20.00 CAN
Trade Paper
1-931847-26-6

Black Bahá'ís in North America represent a wide range of humanity from the unknown to the famous, from the wealthy to the working class. *Lights of the Spirit* includes the powerful stories of butler Robert Turner; Broadway actress Dorothy Champ; upper middle-class couples George and Rosa Shaw (San Francisco), Alexander and Mary Martin (Cleveland), Sadie and Mabry Oglesby (Boston); attorney Louis Gregory; jazz musician Dizzy Gillespie; poet Robert Hayden; and Canadian singer and electrician Eddie Elliot. Who were these individuals, and what attracted them to the Bahá'í Faith? What roles did they play within the Faith and within their respective African-American communities? How did their lives contribute to a community of love and justice wherein true brotherhood would emerge? The answers to these questions and more are answered through historical documents, oral histories, letters, diaries, journals, and essays.

The Divine Art of Living
Compiled by Mabel Hyde Paine, revised by Anne Marie Scheffer
$14.00 / $17.00 CAN
Trade Paper
1-931847-18-5

A compilation of encouraging, positive extracts from Bahá'í scripture that provide an illuminating description of spiritual life and summarize many of the teachings of the Bahá'í Faith. It addresses such topics as learning how to know, love, and trust God; recognizing the purpose of this life; the importance of daily prayer and meditation; and service to mankind. *The Divine Art of Living* is a source of inspiration and encouragement to develop a positive perspective on life.

To view our complete catalog, please visit

Books.Bahai.us